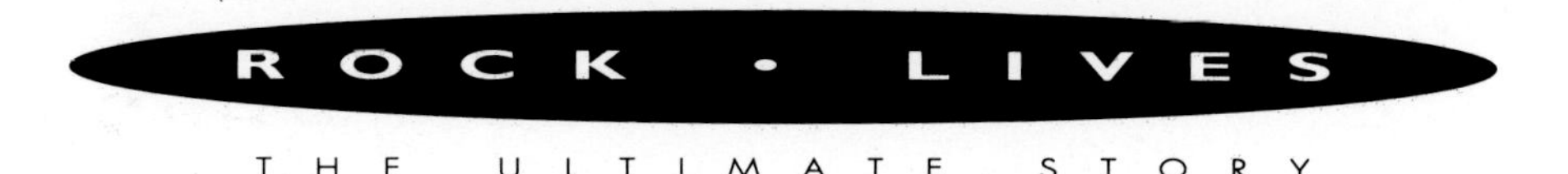

THE ULTIMATE STORY

Robert Plant & Led Zeppelin

Neville Marten and Jeffrey Hudson

Design: Slatter - Anderson
Printed through: World Print, Hong Kong
Cover photograph: Pictorial Press Ltd
Photographs: Neal Preston

Published by castle Communications plc,
A29 Barwell Business Park,
Leatherhead Road, Chessington,
Surrey, KT9 2NY.

ISBN: 1 860740 308

Gods Of Rock In The Beginning...

1968 was a confused year for British popular music; it really didn't know where it was or what it was supposed to be. The Beatles released 'The Beatles' (better known as 'The White Album'), a convoluted package of songs by a group who didn't like itself any more and who obviously felt the strain of working together. It still topped the album chart though. Cliff Richard's *Congratulations* came runner up in the Eurovision Song Contest while the Rolling Stones released 'Beggars Banquet' in reply to their great rivals' white offering; Cream and Hendrix were the big musical thing and the Americans repaid our British Invasion with Flower Power, Bubble Gum and some redeeming brilliance from the talents of Otis Redding, Marvin Gaye, The Supremes, Aretha Franklin and co. Dylan took the No 1 spot in the album chart, but then again so did 'The Sound Of Music', Tom Jones, The Hollies, Andy Williams and The Seekers.

Psychedelia was still tripping along, with Traffic and Procol Harum noodling nonsense lyrics over organically inspired musical arrangements, while a young Pink Floyd rode high on their surprise Top 10 hit, *See Emily Play*.

The Fab Four saw out 68 as they saw it in, at No 1. This time it was with 'Abbey Road', a more satisfying and cohesive effort than the roundly criticised 'White Album' (even though much of said cohesion was supplied by producer George Martin).

And that was about it, musically. Oh, except that The Yardbirds split up. The Yardbirds were a

RIGHT PICTURE

It's just a little get together at my place...

MAIN PICTURE

In the light...

moderately successful R&B outfit, more notorious at the time for their baby blond, bongo playing vocalist Keith Relf than for including Eric Clapton, Jeff Beck and the successful session guitarist Jimmy Page in their various lineups. They also had a few contracted dates left in the book, notably a short tour of Scandinavia; both Page and the group's manager Peter Grant were anxious to fulfil their obligations, feelings which coincided with Jimmy's desire to get out of a session scene which was becoming progressively more stifling with each monotonous take.

The Yardbirds were a London band and Page was a London guitarist. Among literally hundreds of his anonymous sessions (backing musicians were rarely credited) were tracks by Donovan, The Kinks, Dusty Springfield, Cliff Richard, Val Doonican, Van Morrison's band Them and Dave Berry. In fact it has been stated that another 60s session ace, Big Jim Sullivan, played the mournful guitar on Berry's *The Crying Game*, but Big Jim told us that it was Jimmy: "I played rhythm guitar," he admitted candidly. The eerie sound emanates from a DeArmond volume/tone pedal, the precursor to the wah-wah, first used on record by Eric Clapton but more readily associated with the late Jimi Hendrix.

Another musician making waves on the London session scene was bassist, organist and musical

LEFT PICTURE

Jonesy receives a sitting ovation.

TOP RIGHT PICTURE

JPJ at the mighty wurlitzer.

arranger John Paul Jones. In fact Jones and Page had worked together on many occasions and were both becoming bored with the never ending treks down back alleys and basement stairways, as well as the limited musical input they were allowed (and the total lack of credit where it was often due). So when the prospect of a possible new band came up during a break in the recording of Donovan's *Hurdy Gurdy Man*, Jones instantly put himself forward for the post. "John simply wanted to be part of a group of musicians who could lay down some good things," insisted Page; "he had proper music training and he had quite brilliant ideas. I jumped at the chance of getting him." Jimmy and Peter Grant, of course, were also aware of those outstanding Yardbirds dates, which were contracted and so had to be met.

Locating the right singer and drummer was to be the next stumbling block. And Page and Plant required only the best. Terry Reid was the initial choice of vocalist for the 'New Yardbirds' but Terry had just signed a solo deal with legendary pop hitmaker Mickie Most and so declined the position. He did however know someone who'd be perfect. His name was Robert Plant and a trip was arranged to see the singer in action.

Page travelled to the Midlands to witness the performance. Hobbstweedle, the band in question, were performing at a Birmingham teacher training college to an audience comprising a dozen or so students, each of them more interested in booze than blues. "I thought Robert was fantastic," said Jimmy later; "I realised that his voice had an exceptional and very distinctive quality."

Hobbstweedle's blues based material showcased Plant's range and scope enough for Jimmy to invite the vocalist to visit his home at Pangbourne, by the River Thames, to discuss things further. They sat and they sang and they played and they clicked. Robert was keen to tackle something with real prospects; a project which he could influence from the very beginning. In Page he also saw the perfect musical foil; someone with a broad knowledge of many styles and seemingly more than proficient in all of them. Plant also knew the perfect skinsman: John 'Bonzo' Bonham!
Jimmy had already seen Bonham in action,

bashing away manically but musically behind Plant at the Birmingham college gig, and so knew he was no slouch. But if Page did need any convincing, Robert was adamant: "We needed a drummer who was a good timekeeper and who really laid it down, and the only one I knew was the one I'd been working with for years."

But the decision was not so simple for Bonham. He had only recently begun earning good money with the American singer Tim Rose, and offers were in the wings from both Chris Farlowe (who'd already had chart success with Jagger and Richards' *Out Of Time,* on which Page had played) and the up and coming Joe Cocker (on whose cover of The Beatles' *With A Little Help From My Friends* Jimmy had also supplied lead guitar). Eventually, according to Bonham, it was the choice and quality of music that the new group was likely to play – along with Page's pedigree – that swayed him. "And it paid off," he stated dryly.

How the band arrived at its name is the stuff of rock legend. While doing sessions for Jeff Beck's B-side to *Hi Ho Silver Lining* – a Page tune entitled *Beck's Bolero* and Jimi Hendrix's favourite piece of guitar playing – the idea for a supergroup was first mooted. The group would comprise Page and Beck on guitars, The Who's Keith Moon on drums, sessionist Nicky Hopkins on piano and another Who member John Entwistle on bass and vocals. Traffic's Stevie Winwood and The Small Faces' Steve Marriott were also considered, but a 'broken fingers' threat from Marriott's manager soon put paid to that idea! Both Moon and Entwistle have laid claim to the initial phrase which spawned the name, "It'll go down like a lead balloon." But Page maintains it originated with Moon – in which lays a certain irony, considering the deaths of both drummers some years later. Manager Peter Grant, astute as ever, quickly saw the potential for mispronunciation – ie 'leed' instead of 'lead' – simply removed the 'a' and with the stroke of a pen created a phenomenon which would go on to storm the stages of the world, break box office and chart records everywhere and, without overstating the case, invent rock music as we know it today.

MAIN PICTURE

Jimmy's Botswana brown '59 Telecaster is a firm favourite.

TOP PICTURE

Jonesy makes a grand entrance.

James Patrick Page 9 January 1944, Heston, Middlesex

When Mrs Page was delivered of a Capricorn son that cold winter's day, London was still war torn, rationed, blacked out and battered. Little could she have guessed that 25 years later the boy would be the most revered player of an instrument not even yet invented: the solid bodied electric guitar. But young Jimmy, slightly frail and a little prone to illness, would grow up to be the quintessential rock guitar god, his Gibson Les Paul Standard slung low over his hips, face contorted, fingers dragging every drop of feeling from his instrument.

Although born in Heston, a southwest suburb of London alongside Heathrow Airport, Page spent much of his youth at an uncle's farm in Northamptonshire, before the family moved to Epsom, Surrey when he was aged eight. The guitar entered his life at around 13, although the initial indifference shown to the instrument by the lad belied what was to come. "It was sitting around our living room for weeks and weeks," confessed Page, "but I wasn't interested." Then one day Jimmy heard the enthralling strains of Scotty Moore, Bill Black and DJ Fontana laying down the awesome feel behind Elvis Presley's acoustic guitar on *Baby Let's Play House*: "I heard that record and wanted to be part of it," emphasised Page; "I heard that acoustic guitar, slap bass and electric guitar – three instruments and a voice – and they generated so much energy... That's when I started."

ABOVE PICTURE

"I always thought the good thing about guitar was that they didn't teach it in school."

MAIN PICTURE

"And she's buying a stairway to Heaven." Jimmy and his unmistakeable Gibson EDS1275 twin neck.

The fact is sometimes overlooked that Jimmy adored the acoustic guitar with the same passion he displayed towards his electrics. But not only was he fascinated by different tunings and playing styles, he would also adapt versions of other acoustic players' pieces to suit his own preferred way of playing; thus was born many a Led Zeppelin song later on.

Page's prime influence on the acoustic was Bert Jansch, "a real dream weaver," as he put it. Jansch, along with John Renbourn and Davey Graham, led a significant 60s folk guitar revival. But not for them the unsophisticated strumming or simple fingerpicking styles of others; the three players contrived clever tunings and fingerings to create sounds which fascinated many musicians – a young Mike Oldfield was experiencing the same thrill that would inspire Page.

It should also be understood that at this time in England the guitar was a very down market instrument; something a coffee bar layabout might dabble with, but nothing that an intelligent young man with prospects should have anything to do with. So Jimmy's love affair with his guitar inevitably led him into conflict with those who sought to set him on a better course. Every day he'd take it to school and every day it would be confiscated, since young Page insisted on playing the instrument in class (it would be handed back each evening when school finished). But Jimmy revelled in the rebelliousness of it all: "I always thought the good thing about guitar was that they didn't teach it in school," he affirmed. "Teaching myself to play was the first and most important part of my education."

Unlike many, if not most professional musicians, Page never had a 'proper' job. The nearest he came to that, he says, was interviewing for a post as a laboratory assistant: "But I chose The Crusaders instead, until my health started playing up."

The Crusaders were actually Neil Christian And The Crusaders, an R&B band specialising in raunchy Chuck Berry and Bo Diddley songs and it was from this platform of local notoriety that Jimmy was eventually to launch himself into the session scene. He was making something of a reputation for himself and many great guitarists would talk later of having seen Page, or heard about his astonishing prowess during this period.

The band realised the star they had in Jimmy and had him performing all manner of antics on stage – bending over backwards until his head touched the floor, all the while pulling out show stopping licks from his guitar. On top of this the gigs were gruelling; driving up and down the country (motorways didn't exist) for little money or recognition, sleeping in the band wagon and generally living on the hoof. So, inevitably, Jimmy's less than robust health gave out. The debilitating and energy sapping illness glandular fever got its grip on the guitarist and after two years with The Crusaders he was forced to quit.

Here Jimmy's life took a temporary change of direction. He had always loved art and painting

MAIN PICTURE

Page was persuaded to try the bowing technique by a session violinist.

and so decided to enroll as a student at Sutton College of Art. He seriously believed that this was where his future lay, but still spent every available moment playing, or hanging out and sitting in at clubs like Richmond's famous stomping ground for musicians, The Crawdaddy; London's Marquee or

Eel Pie Island at Twickenham. In the end the contest between art and music was a one sided affair and Jimmy was soon back playing full time. Page himself put it down to the fact that during the previous years the British public was uninterested in the type of music he wanted to play. "Then, a year later everything started to happen," he explained. "The Rolling Stones broke through and there were the Liverpool and R&B scenes coming together. I enjoyed playing and the R&B revival restored my faith in pop music."

The year was 1963 and Jimmy was on the lookout for work, although in reality most of it was to come to him. During one of his sit-ins at The Marquee he had been spotted by producer Mike Leander. Leander booked him to play on the instrumental single *Diamonds* by Jet Harris and Tony Meehan. Harris and Meehan had originally been bassist and drummer in The Shadows but parted with the group to form their own duo. So Page's first serious session became a No 1 smash, although

RIGHT PICTURE

Grant and Plant.

MAIN PICTURE

"I just sat next to Pagey while he was playing it through. It took a little working out, it was a very fluid, unnaturally easy track." Plant, on writing the lyrics to "Stairway...".

nobody knew Jimmy had played a note on the record. Meehan played the melody on what sounded like a six string bass, although it was actually a regular guitar tuned down; Jimmy probably provided the strummed rhythm part.

Thus began a career as sideman to all and sundry. It is impossible to say which tracks Page actually played on, or which solos he performed. Even Jimmy doesn't remember. But much controversy surrounds who actually handled the solos on The Kinks' early singles, *All Day And All Of The Night* and *You Really Got Me*. Many guitar aficionados swear they can tell it's Page on *All Day And All Of The Night* and that The Kinks' young guitarist Dave Davies was then incapable of such dexterity.

Jimmy has apparently never confirmed himself as the guitarist and Davies remains quiet.

A bootleg album exists of Jimmy's session days. Entitled 'James Patrick Page: Session Man', it was originally released in 1979 and contains many previously unheard tracks. As a Page fanatic's collectable, the record is a valuable icon, but as a study in the works of this great player it cannot be recommended. Songs are mainly by unheard of artists and the guitar is anything but prominent and nothing like the James Patrick Page we would probably all prefer to hear.

Nevertheless, Jimmy will consider himself fortunate to have gained such a magnificent grounding in so many musical styles. Never a great reader of music he must have been thrown in at the deep end on dozens of occasions, simply letting his devil may care attitude and natural musical brilliance pull him through. Listen to some of his early Zeppelin solos to hear a guitarist on the edge of his abilities but with the guts and confidence to simply go for it.

Jimmy was also financially well rewarded for his efforts as a sessioneer, earning many times more than would have been possible under normal circumstances. He became a well dressed, Beau Brummel-esque character, obviously a dedicated leader of fashion but also adopting the Carnabecian image of the time. Jimmy always looked dapper and coiffured. Check out photos of Page and you will invariably notice the details: a cravat, a high buttoned collar, double breasted coat, a kerchief, a button hole, satin or velvet lapels. Here was a man who liked detail – perfection even – someone who, given the opportunity to shape the destiny of his own band, might actually come up with something quite extraordinary.

The Yardbirds

The Yardbirds' first successful lineup featured Keith Relf (vocals, bongos), Eric Clapton (lead guitar), Chris Dreja (rhythm guitar), Paul Samwell-Smith (bass) and Jim McCarty (drums). The band enjoyed a terrific local reputation around Richmond, where they took over The Rolling Stones' residency at The Crawdaddy. They also had considerable chart success, with Top 10 singles *For Your Love, Heart Full Of Soul, Evil Hearted You, Shapes Of Things* and *Over Under Sideways Down*. But the internal politics of the group were such that things in the guitar department remained volatile.

Clapton was at this point the guitarist with the highest reputation in London. And this was the time when the infamous 'Clapton Is God' graffiti made its entrance and Eric gained the nickname Slowhand, due to the speed of his fingers. But he was soon to be tempted away from the band with an offer no white middle class blues purist could refuse; John Mayall asked him to join his Bluesbreakers. But this was not before Eric had recorded *For Your Love*, which he despised with a vengeance for its luke warm poppiness.

Jeff Beck tells an amusing story about Clapton at this time. It is included here simply to point out that within a couple of square miles, and at one particular moment in time, three of the world's greatest blues/rock guitarists were learning and plying their trade. And they would all serve time in The Yardbirds.

Jeff was already aware of Eric: "All everyone kept saying to me was, 'Clapton, Clapton, Clapton' and I started to get a bit worried about how good the guy was," but Beck had never heard his rival play. Jeff and Jimmy were already friends and the two

measured up well as rivals, but the thought of an unknown 'God' who could apparently beat them both was the stuff of bad dreams. Beck: "Anyway, one night we were coming back from a gig and had stopped to get a burger or something. The guy on the burger stand had a little transistor radio blaring away and all of a sudden *For Your Love* came on and one of the group said, 'That's Clapton!' Well, apart from the bit in the middle where he plays a little 12 bar break there's no guitar on the record at all. So I thought to myself, 'Well, if that's Clapton, I've got nothing to worry about.' It was only later that I found out how good he actually was."

So Eric left to join Mayall's Bluesbreakers, leaving a hole that could only be filled by another formidable player. Jimmy was offered the position but turned it down, instead recommending his pal, the moody, unreliable but inspirational Jeff Beck. Beck continued in the band and produced one of the best guitar solos of the 60s on the group's No 3 single *Shapes Of Things*, a sort of pop-rock protest number. Page knew the band well and was actually on hand (he'd gone to the gig with Beck) when Paul Samwell Smith's latest disagreement over a rather ramshackle and drunken performance by Relf caused him to leave the group, at the same time creating a vacancy in the bass player's chair.

MAIN PICTURE

"The manager just told me I couldn't sing." Plant on getting fired from The Band of Joy.

"I'd never played one before," tells Jimmy of his first run-in with a bass guitar. But a couple of hours' rehearsal was all it took for a natural like him to pass for a 'real' bassist at the next Marquee gig.

Page remained on bass for some time, until Chris Dreja swapped over from rhythm guitar. Audiences were now presented with the doubly whammy of Beck and Page on dual lead. "The idea was for Jeff and me to get a stereo guitar sound," explained Jimmy. "With two lead guitars it worked really well. Lots of people have done it since but I think we must have been the first."

British and American tours were taking their toll on the health and nerves of certain band members. On one gig, Jeff Beck collapsed and Jimmy switched back to bass; on another, Beck simply walked out and was asked not to return. Here, Page the arbitrator came to the fore, persuading the band not to fall apart. He explained that there was a good future to be had in a group with a track record such as theirs.

Another momentous change occurred at this time; The Yardbirds and their long time manager Simon Napier Bell went their separate ways. Apparently the group were tired of traipsing around the world, wearing themselves out, making enemies of friends and returning with hardly a bean to show for it all.

Peter Grant was to be a different kind of manager. He quickly arranged a tour of Australia and the band realised at last that there was money to be made in the music business (under Napier-Bell they had apparently toured America for a month, undertaken a Rolling Stones UK tour and come home with £118.00 each).

As Grant took over the band's management, Mickie Most accepted the job of recording the next Yardbirds' album, 'Little Games'. Of course, Jimmy had already worked with Most as a musician, and Jeff Beck's *Hi Ho Silver Lining* and *Blue* were Mickie Most projects too. Grant and Most had also shared an office next door to Stones manager Andrew Loog Oldham's Immediate Records, where Page had spent some time as house producer. Jimmy left Immediate when the label released some questionable jam sessions which he had recorded at home with Eric Clapton. It was just a few tracks buried on a blues compilation album, with Jimmy playing mainly rhythm guitar and Eric soloing a little too politely over it. Jimmy was mortified when the label concocted some liner notes which they attributed to him.

But 'Little Games' wasn't going well. Most, it seems, saw it as a British flower power statement while the band had different and opposing ideas of their own. According to Page, Mickie would not allow time for extra takes or overdubs, making the whole thing sound less than professional; the last thing The Yardbirds themselves would want at this point in their careers. "Mickie Most was basically interested in singles," commented Page, "and didn't believe it was worth the time to do the tracks right on the album."

Eventually 'Little Games' was only released in America, but managed to reach a paltry No 80 on the *Billboard* album chart. A recording was made of a concert in New York, potentially for release as a live album, but Jimmy and the band were unimpressed on hearing the tapes and so the project never saw the light of day.

In July 1968 the band decided to pull the shutters down on The Yardbirds. "I tried desperately to keep them together," recalled Jimmy. "The gigs were there, but Keith in particular would not take them very seriously. It was a real shame. The group were almost ashamed of the very name, though I don't know why. They were a great band. I was never ashamed of playing in The Yardbirds."

Along with Jim McCarty, Keith Relf went on to form the successful folk rock group Renaissance, but died tragically, electrocuted by his own guitar, in 1976. Dreja took up photography and supplied the shots for the sleeve of the first album from Page's new outfit, a group who called themselves Led Zeppelin.

MAIN PICTURE

John Paul Jones plays an unusual Fender Bass IV.

Robert Anthony Plant 20 August 1948, West Bromwich, Staffordshire

After the birth of their son the Plant family moved closer to Birmingham, to Kidderminster in the West Midlands. As a teenager young Robert received no encouragement from his parents when seeking to join the burgeoning rock'n'roll movement. In fact, like Page he found the whole thing was frowned upon from every quarter, and so decided to leave home at age 16, search for a decent band and if he hadn't made it by 20, simply give up.

The previous year Robert had discovered traditional blues and developed something of a passion for singing it. He spent a lot of his spare time at the Seven Stars Blues Club in Stourbridge, where he became captivated by local musician Terry Foster. "Terry was an incredible eight string guitarist," he enthused. "Instead of playing in the normal way, he used to play like Big Joe Williams, with the instrument half on his lap. He was a horrible bloke at times, but when I was 15 I fell immediately under his spell." Foster introduced Plant to more blues and helped nurture an appreciation. Robert loved the lonesome vocal styles of Robert Johnson, Sonny Boy Williamson, Muddy Waters, Snooks Elgin and Howlin' Wolf and spent hours copying their phrasing, but mating this to the physical dynamism of Elvis Presley. A powerful sexual concoction!

PICTURE LEFT

"You see, here I am, the lead singer in Led Zeppelin, and underneath I still enjoy Fairport Convention and Buffalo Springfield."

Plant decided that the life of a chartered accountant – his parents' preferred choice of career – was not for him, figuring that infinitely more reward, fun and girls could be gained by fronting a serious blueswailing band. So after just a fortnight he left his trainee accountant's position and began the rounds of the local bands, including Black Snake Moan, The New Memphis Bluesbreakers, The Crawling King Snakes and The Delta Blues Band. Plant also learned to play the blues harmonica (or harp) around this time, an instrument which fascinated him almost as much as the vocalisations of his Delta heroes.

The Plant vocal style and onstage presence – already including long, blond, flowing locks, the cause of much consternation at home – was taking shape and Robert soon found himself in demand on the Midlands blues scene. "My Dad used to drop me off at the Seven Stars Blues Club and we used to wail away to *Got My Mojo Working* and stuff like that," reported Robert. "Chris Wood [later of Traffic] used to play with us, and Stan Webb [*who formed Chicken Shack*] were in a competing band. The Seven Stars Club was really my initiation."

Plant's first settled group was called Listen, and in 1966 the band were approached by CBS Records, whose scouts had been much impressed by Robert's powerful delivery. Birmingham at this time had become a melting pot for an array of talent, including The Move, The Spencer Davis Group with the fantastic 15 year-old Stevie Winwood on guitar,

organ and vocals, and The Moody Blues. London record company scouts were regularly seen at Midlands gigs, checking out the talent and looking for potential signings. Plant had also become increasingly excited by black soul singers such as Otis Redding and Wilson Pickett, as well as local ska and reggae music, so when CBS signed Listen for a three single deal, the blues element was somewhat diluted. While these recordings possess interesting novelty value, ardent Zeppelin fans would surely find them a musical disappointment. In fact, the records featured only Plant, backed by session musicians; the rest of Listen were not heard. The singles were *You Better Run/Everybody's Gonna Say, Our Song/Laughin', Cryin', Laughin'* and *Long Time Coming/I've Got A Secret.*

Soon after this, Robert formed his first Band Of Joy. "Living near Birmingham," he explained, "I got in with a lot of Jamaicans and I started to like blue beat. It was received with open arms. But as a band we were still learning; the drummer would slow the beat every now and then and the guitarist played a few odd chords." Plant was sacked from that band – "The manager just told me I couldn't sing" – but Band Of Joy number two were soon formed. "The new band decided to have painted faces on stage – before the arrival of The Crazy World Of Arthur Brown. It went all right for a while but we were frightening our audiences to death. It was absurd. But we got in a fantastic guitarist, a good bass player and John Bonham came in on drums."

This Band Of Joy lineup – now called Robert Plant and the Band Of Joy – came closer to success than any other. They played all the prestigious Midlands gigs, supported many big name bands and frequently held residencies down at The Marquee, Speakeasy and Middle Earth clubs. They also recorded a set of demos at Regent Sound studios in London. The tracks included *Hey Joe*, the blues standard made famous by Jimi Hendrix, *Adriatic Sea View*, which was later donated by Plant to Kidderminster College's fund raising effort, and Buffalo Springfield's *For What It's Worth.*

By now Plant had become enchanted with the West Coast sounds of bands like Moby Grape and Buffalo Springfield and was beginning to lose his love of pure blues. The new sounds, based more on American flower power and acid rock than blues, began to find its way into the group's set. "I got hold of a Buffalo Springfield album," recalled Robert. "It was great because it was the kind of music you could leap around to, or you could sit down and just dig it. I thought, 'This is what an audience wants and this is what I want to listen to.' Then I got the first Moby Grape album, which was knockout. The guitar playing and everything was very good; it fitted together so well. I had loved old blues, but all of a sudden I couldn't listen to old blues any more. It was really a big change – now I was sobbing to Arthur Lee and Love doing *Forever Changes."*

But in fact Band Of Joy's brand of acid rock, ska and blues proved not to be what audiences wanted and the group never secured the record deal which many felt that they deserved. So, finally, in early spring of 1968 the members went their separate ways, with drummer Bonham going off to work with Tim Rose and Robert returning to London, still determined to make it before he hit 20 – he had but a few months left to go.

Plant was on the loose again, but not for long. Alexis Korner, father of British blues and mentor of many aspiring young musicians had seen Robert performing at The Speakeasy and suggested the two worked together. Unfortunately the pair's teaming was an on and off, hit and miss affair, although it lasted about a year. The two did get some music onto tape though – one track, *Operator*, recorded under the name Duo, emerged many years later on an Alexis Korner anthology. But Robert could not afford to stay with Alexis, since Alexis could hardly afford to pay him.

The Move's manager Tony Secunda then heard Plant's Band Of Joy demo and persuaded him to record an audition tape for Regal Zonophone boss Denny Cordell. Cordell, though impressed with Robert's vocal prowess, rejected him on the basis that the label could sustain no new acts – not to mention the fact that he was concentrating on a young Joe Cocker, who was just breaking into the big time.

So it was back to the Midlands again for Plant, back to playing one nighters with various local outfits – including one called Hobbstweedle, a band that also featured John Bonham on drums.

MAIN PICTURE

"I can only think that we were aware of dynamics at a time when everyone else was into that drawn out, West Coast Style of playing."

John Henry Bonham 31 May 1948, Redditch, Worcestershire

"It wasn't until my father died that I actually decided to concentrate on drums; his death was what made my decision. From when I was about four I just remember being taught; there was a kit there as long as I can remember. It was an old Beatles-type kit; actually more of a Buddy Rich setup; it had the ride cymbal coming out of the bass drum, a little 18 inch bass drum. He put it in the bedroom one Christmas morning and I remember getting up and going boom crash crash crash on it. But from the age of about five or six I could play a beat."

John Bonham describing his days as a fledgling drummer? It certainly could be, such was the passion shown at a similarly early age for the art of percussion. But no, those words were uttered by Bonham's son Jason in 1992, now a successful musician in his own right and speaking 13 years after the death of his father, perhaps the greatest and certainly the most expensive drum tutor in the world.

John 'Bonzo' Bonham's mother knew that her own boy was destined to become a drummer, since apparently he attacked her kitchen pots and saucepans with cruel enthusiasm. This power would become a Bonham trademark. In fact son Jason would later tell of how a few minutes of Dad on one of his own kits would invariably render some part of

ABOVE PICTURE

"He was extremely inventive, more so than any other drummer I'd heard." Page on first hearing Bonham.

MAIN PICTURE

"We used to wear purple jackets with vevet lapels." Bonzo, recalling his days with Terry Webb and the Spiders.

LED ZEPPELIN
69

it lame, wounded or indeed a hopeless casualty. But mated to Bonham's unusual strength was a rare musicality; the ability to gel with a band, to tie the musicians together and propel them through a song in unique style.

Back when John was a mere five years old he would practise on any drum shaped object, adapting a variety of jars and tins for his use. He had a bath salts container with wires attached to the bottom, as a sort of makeshift snare: "And a round coffee tin with a loose wire fixed to it," he added. Here again the wire created the snare effect. When the boy was 10 years old his mother – perhaps fearful for the longevity of her kitchenware – bought him a real snare drum. This wasn't much but it was John's practice kit until age 15, when he received his first full set, a present from his father. "It was prehistoric," recounted Bonham, "mostly rust." But it served Bonzo until he could leave school, begin work in his father's building business, buy a kit of his own and begin his quest for the big time.

Terry Webb And The Spiders were hardly that – "We used to wear purple jackets with velvet lapels," winced Bonzo later – but the band gave the drummer some much needed experience. He soon moved on to enjoy stints with groups such as A Way Of Life, The Crawling King Snakes (with one Robert Plant on vocals) and The Nicky James

MAIN PICTURE

Starship Enterprise.

Movement. According to Bonham, James was a fantastic singer; the only problem in this band was one of gear. "We had so much of the equipment on hire purchase," he laughed, "that we'd get stopped at night on the way back from a gig and they'd take back all the PA."

Another problem was a lack of songwriting in the band. The Nicky James Movement was purely a covers outfit and in those days, the middle 60s, originality was the key to success, especially with inventive writers like Roy Wood of The Move and Stevie Winwood of The Spencer Davis group beginning to make waves on the Birmingham scene. "But I was so keen to play," disclosed Bonham, "that I'd have played for nothing." Which is exactly what he did do for a while, with the help and financial support of his father and the understanding of his wife Pat, who he had married when aged just 17. "I swore to Pat that I'd give up drumming when we got married, but every night I'd come home and just sit down at the drums. I'd be miserable if I didn't."

After a spell with Steve Brett And The Mavericks came another stint in a band with singer Robert Plant. This time it was The Band Of Joy. Bonham remained in this group for two years, until in early

68 they called it a day for financial and musical reasons. But not before they had toured in support of American folk rock artist Tim Rose. Rose was to remember the drummer whose power and soul had helped lift the group to unexpected heights. As The Band Of Joy came to an end Bonzo was offered the chance to tour again with Rose, this time in his backing band and, for once in his musical career, on real wages. £40 was a handsome salary in 1968, ample to support a family in some comfort and enough to impart a rare sense of security in a drummer who had known nothing but struggle and hardship, and who would surely have given up were it not for the aid of his family.

But it never rains, it pours. No sooner had Bonzo settled into his position of security than the offers started pouring in. Bonham had gained something of a reputation as a hard hitter (the same reputation had earlier got him banned from clubs in the area, due to the sheer volume of his playing) and two up and coming rock acts, eager to add some weight to their lineups, were after him. Joe Cocker and Chris Farlowe were both tempting propositions: Farlowe already enjoyed some measure of chart success and was also rated by the musical cognoscenti; Cocker was being promoted by The Move's manager Tony Secunda and his prospects looked set to soar.

MAIN PICTURE

"There are times when you sit down and say, 'I wanna go home'."

And then the wild card was played. Flamboyant Band Of Joy frontman Robert Plant had become attached to Bonham's style of playing. So much so that when he and session guitar ace Jimmy Page got together and set out their stall for a new, super version of Page's old band The Yardbirds, it was Bonzo's name that found its way to the top of their list of prospective drummers. Page said of Bonham later: "I couldn't believe the way he was living his music. He was extremely inventive, more so than any other drummer I'd heard. I knew he'd be incredible."

But the decision was difficult for Bonzo: he was on regular money for the first time in his life; his job was secure and he felt he should stick out the position with Rose for as long as it was there (after all, the singer was sure to return to the States at some point and might not take Bonham with him); the offers from Cocker and Farlowe looked equally tempting, if not more so, for perhaps The Yardbirds' time had been and gone. But Plant and manager Peter Grant applied the pressure – Bonzo reputedly ignored 40 telegrams from Grant before replying! In the end it was a combination of factors that swayed him, plus a gut feeling that told him this was it. Bonham: "I had so much to consider. It wasn't a question of who had the right prospects, but which was going to be the right kind of stuff. I already knew from playing in The Band Of Joy with Robert what he liked, and I knew what Jimmy was into. I just decided I liked that sort of music better."

John Paul Jones 3 January 1946, Sidcup, Kent

John Baldwin, or John Paul Jones as he came to call himself, could hardly fail to become a musician of some note. Unlike the inhibited Page, Plant and Bonham, who managed it through either determination, sheer talent or both, Jones's parents were highly creative, musical people who nurtured their son's inherent musical interest. John Paul's mother was a successful singer and dancer, while his father was pianist and arranger in such legendary British bands as Ambrose and his orchestra.

A self taught pianist, John Paul read music well and showed a natural aptitude, soon helping out on the organ at the local church.

He went to Christ College at Blackheath in south east London and, through listening to the track You Can't Sit Down by the jazz guitarist Phil Upchurch, became turned on to the bass. "It has an incredible bass solo," said Jones of the song;

MAIN PICTURE

Jones playing 12 string.

"it was simple musically, but the record had an incredible amount of balls."

Jones joined several local rock bands during his teenage years. He also formed a successful functions duo with his father, which kept the pair busy during the holiday periods. John Paul would also gain much experience in the art of musical arranging from this partnership, but his abilities and drive were such that he would soon find himself entering the hectic world of the 60s London session scene.

But before this, and as a matter of complete coincidence, he joined a hit making instrumental band, just as their instrumental Diamonds was at No 1 on the UK hit parade. Diamonds you may remember, had a young Jimmy Page making his recording session debut on rhythm guitar. As John recalled recently: "It was a band that not too many people will have heard of, called the Jet Harris And Tony Meehan Band.

There used to be a kind of convention every Monday where a bunch of musicians would hang around Archers Street, just off Shaftesbury Avenue in London, to see if there were any faces you could recognise and try and get work with. I went continually to Archers Street, because although I had a band it wasn't getting any work. I had left school at 16 and it was looking like I might have to get a proper job! One day I saw Jet Harris. I'd heard he'd made a record, left The Shadows and was getting together with Tony Meehan. I said do you want a bass player and he said no, he was already fixed up, but recommended me for another gig, with The Jet Blacks."

Jones auditioned for The Jet Blacks and got the job. "But Jet had sent one of his spies to the audition," continues John Paul, "realised I was the better player and so did a crafty swap on the night. I ended up with Jet and Tony, which gave me my first break with a band that had No 1 records and concerts where the curtain opens up and the screaming starts."

Jones's early bass guitars were made by Burns of London (who also built special guitars for The Shadows and whose founder, Jim Burns, became known as the British Leo Fender), although he later became best known for his work with Fender's own Jazz bass. "I had the Burns bass because I couldn't afford a Fender," confessed Jones. "I'd like to say that I tried lots of basses before buying the Fender Jazz, but in actual fact it was the only one in the shop!"

The Harris-Meehan hit making formula was not one which successfully rode the tide of Beatlemania that had fully gripped the country by 1964. So the band folded and Jones was left to pursue a solo career. "After I left Jet and Tony I became Andrew Oldham's musical director, so I was arranging quite a lot, although I still did mainly sessions on bass." John Paul also released a single of his own; like Jet Harris, using six string bass. "Yes, it was called *Baja*. I was supposed to have a solo career and become the next Jet Harris," he admitted, "beginning with this instrumental single, but I was still doing sessions and arranging, then more sessions..."

Tony Meehan himself became an in house producer for Decca Records and used Jones and other members of the Harris-Meehan band for as many sessions as possible. So before long John Paul's services as a bassist were much in demand on the London circuit.

In fact by the mid to late 60s he was the highest paid session musician around. "At that time I was spending £100 a week on cab fares alone," recalls Jones, "just getting from session to session. I was making a fortune, especially as the shops weren't open when I was free!" Included in these sessions were many jobs with the young guitar star of the London studios, Jimmy Page. In fact Jones was responsible for several arrangements on The Yardbirds' final album together, 'Little Games' and of course Donovan's hit single *Hurdy Gurdy Man*, where the seeds for a new group were first sewn.

Jones's influences on bass guitar were many and various, but Motown's extraordinary in house bassist James Jamerson was his prime inspiration. "Everybody from that time was influenced in a way," explained John Paul, "because it was only on Tamla records that you heard the bass; everybody else either mixed it badly or played it badly. On Tamla records they would put drums on one side of the mix, strings and trumpets on the other and voice and bass in the middle, so you could pick it out." The Motown mixing technique was something Jones tried to adhere to in his own productions: "If you get the voice and bass sorted out," he asserts, "everything else kind of falls into place."

By 68 the quantity and indeed the quality of some of the work Jones was required to undertake was, in much the same way as Page, seriously getting him down. "I was doing 20 sessions and 10 arrangements a week," he sighed, "the highest paid, youngest session musician in England. But I was going completely bananas. I'd read that Jimmy Page was forming a band and my wife [*he was by now married with two children*] said, 'You're going to have to do something, why not give them a call?' So I called Jimmy who told me he was just off to Birmingham to see a singer. Jimmy came back and said they were great, so did I want to do it? I said, 'Yes', then he added, 'We'll have to put them on wages because Bonzo's making £100 a week and he won't leave Tim Rose'. I agreed, and we put them on wages. The rest is history..."

Take Off Working Up A Set

"The name was just a joke in England," tells Page. "We really had a bad time. They just wouldn't accept anything new. It had to be The New Yardbirds, not Led Zeppelin." Such was the antipathy that greeted news of the new act in its own country. Zeppelin couldn't get work in the UK and it almost seemed to Jones, Page and company that they were being treated as some kind of embarrassing joke.

But having spent early September rehearsing together in London, running through a mixture of tunes old and new, borrowed and blue, it was obvious the new lineup was going to gel. Fears that Page, the most famous of the four, might play the prima donna and seek centre stage were instantly dispelled. As John Paul Jones put it: "Any feelings of competition within the group vanished after one number."

MAIN PICTURE

Ooh yeah, ooh yeah..."

RIGHT PICTURE

Bonzo: an Englishman abroad."

So the rehearsals continued and the music became tighter. A repertoire was beginning to take shape; new songs were finely honed, others were resurrected from the old Yardbirds stage show and given new treatments; old blues numbers were

revamped and came out sounding fresh and exciting. On the following album, the original writers of some of Zep's blues 'quotes' would call "foul", and go on to receive both musical credit and financial acknowledgement. But for now Zeppelin were becoming a reality, soon to put their music to the test, both live and in the recording studio.

The already scheduled 10 date tour of Scandinavia was to be Bonham's first trip in an aeroplane. He was nervous, but only slightly more so than the rest of the band. Zeppelin was

Page's baby and much was resting on his shoulders. Plant had thrown it all in and moved from the Midlands for a final fling at success. Jones was relinquishing a fantastic living as top session bassist and arranger and Bonham had turned down seemingly surefire success. And all for what? Accompanied by manager Peter Grant they would find out soon enough.

Before they left, however, the band were booked to back American singer PJ Proby (hits including *Somewhere, Maria* and *Hold Me*, but probably best known for splitting his trousers on stage) on a track for his album 'Three Week Hero'. The group played with manic power on *Jim's Blues*, surprising even the larger than life Proby; Plant played blues harp and the record is now a collector's item. Scandinavia went extraordinarily well, considering the band members had previously not played together in anger, and that the music was new to them and even newer to the wide eyed Swedes and Norwegians who could hardly have understood the momentous nature of what they were witnessing. Grant became morose and worried before the first gig on 14th September. "I kept thinking, 'What have we got into here?'" he recalled of those nerve wracking moments before the band came on stage. "I can't say all the notes were correct," he continued, "but the feeling was there and the magic was there. I knew we were right."

Zeppelin arrived back in London ready to commit their new set of songs to tape. The Scandinavian outing had been the perfect opportunity to whip the songlist into shape. And the new live set was to become the basis for the first LP. The tour had also given Plant, Page and the band the advantage of seeing which songs fired up an audience and which ones left it cool. The track sequence for the new record was quite possibly also guided by what combinations had worked well on stage in Scandinavia.

After the tour it was decided to go for broke, drop the New Yardbirds name and call the band by the title finally agreed during rehearsals. By this time Jimmy couldn't have cared what they were called; he simply wanted to get on with it and make some music. "You can call it The Vegetables or The Potatoes," he said. In fact, The Mad Boys, The Mad Dogs and The Whoopie Cushions were all at least semi-seriously considered.

And so it was that Jimmy Page, Robert Plant, John Bonham and John Paul Jones entered Olympic Studios in London to record the group's first album: 'Led Zeppelin'.

TOP LEFT PICTURE

Double – neck? Pah! JPJ with his three necked Manson acoustic.

RIGHT PICTURE

Misty Mountain Hop?

'Led Zeppelin' Maiden Voyage

Surprising as it may seem now, for their debut vinyl offering Led Zeppelin had no recording contract. So Jimmy Page and Peter Grant put up the cash to pay for studio time at Olympic. The amount is paltry and ridiculous by today's standards, but 'Led Zeppelin' cost a mere £1,782 to record, due to the professionalism of the players involved and the fact that their material was being laid down more or less live. The whole thing took an incredible 30 hours to complete (at that exact moment Simon and Garfunkel were labouring over their next single, *The Boxer;* which would take a reputed 100 hours). As Page explained at the time: "It was easy because we had a repertoire of numbers all worked out and we just went into the studio and did it. I suppose it was the fact that we were confident and prepared to make things flow smoothly. As it happened, we recorded the songs almost exactly as we'd been doing them live."

MAIN PICTURE

The smile remains the same...

CENTRE PICTURE

Jones: the quiet, moody one.

During this same period Page managed to find time to fit in a couple of sessions; with Al Stewart on *Love Chronicles* and the momentous *With A Little Help From My Friends* by Joe Cocker.

Glyn Johns, who had worked with many of the famous names of the 60s, was engineer on the album and Page took on the role of producer. Jimmy's thousands of hours spent playing and contributing ideas to the arrangements of other artists' songs will have proved invaluable in this. Of course John Paul Jones was an old studio hand too, and although Plant and Bonham were fledglings by comparison, with experience limited to a few demos and unsuccessful single attempts, their confidence and proficiency was enough to see them through. "It was a very exciting record to cut," recalled engineer Johns. "I had never heard arrangements of that ilk and certainly never heard a band play in that way before. It was just unbelievable, and when you're in a studio with something as creative as that you can't help but feed off it."

In order that studio time was not mis-spent or frittered away in needless jam sessions, Page took the project by the reins and insisted upon a sense of order during the proceedings. The sounds on the record were to be raw and real, Page experimenting with placing microphones at a distance from the drums and amplifiers, rather than the 'close miking' which had become *de rigueur* by then. As Jimmy said, "I was into ambience. I wanted to hear the drums sound like drums and realised that if you close miked them they tended to sound like cardboard boxes. My studio maxim was 'distance makes depth'." Johns was later surprised when Jimmy took the finished master tapes to New York to add, in his view, senseless and naive mixing ideas.

The record opens with *Good Times Bad Times.* A very unbluesy start to the album, this wonderful pop rock song features hooks to grab the listener's attention from start to finish. Jones's Motown influence is evident in the warm and melodic bass riffing heard here. The arrangement is more structured than many of the songs on the album, with a distinct verse, chorus format and with Plant's vocal excesses tamed – for the time being at least. Harmonies from John and Jimmy, too! Page's first solo on the first track of this first album was to set a familiar scene; a frenzied guitar orgasm, cleverly set up by the producer for maximum effect. Page was often to do this; break the music for a moment, before releasing a rush of notes to lift the song to another level, up another musical gear in fact. This was Jimmy's Fender Telecaster, played through a Leslie organ speaker cabinet for that swirling effect. Particularly wonderful is the bass drum work from Bonham who, in all his time in the band, was never to simply sit there and bash out a beat!

According to both Jimmy and Robert, the largely acoustic *Babe I'm Gonna Leave You* featured the most post production work, in the form of arrangements, overdubs etc. As Page recalled: "Only *Babe I'm Gonna Leave You* was altered, as far as I can remember. Plant went further: "The two of us rearranged *Babe I'm Gonna Leave You*. When we heard it back in the studio we were shaking hands with our brains because it worked out to be so nice." Plant first heard this song, sung by Joan Baez, at his initial get together with Page at the guitarist's Thamesside home. The acoustic guitar is possibly Mickie Most's Gibson J200, an instrument often used by guitarists on Mickie's sessions and almost certainly played by Jimmy many times before. Unfortunately this beautiful piece was stolen from Most's RAK studios some time later and, to the authors' knowledge, has never resurfaced.

MAIN PICTURE

A time of peace and love. . .

The classic A minor with descending bass line chord sequence builds towards the end of the track, with added distorted guitars from Jimmy. This well known sequence is redolent of other tunes, including George Harrison's *While My Guitar Gently Weeps* ('White Album') and Chicago's *25 Or 6 To 4*. The way Page arranged the tune, adding rhythmic changes, stops, starts and instrumental breaks, was perhaps a foretaste of what was to come some three albums later, with *Stairway To Heaven*.

The Willie Dixon/JB Lenoir slow blues *You Shook Me* begins with the thick tone of Page's slide guitar. Not to be confused with the pedal steel which Jimmy added to tracks such as *Your Time Is Gonna Come* and *Babe I'm Gonna Leave You*, this was either Page's Fender Telecaster (bridge pickup with the treble turned off) or perhaps his old Gibson Les Paul Standard. The sliding note effect is achieved by running a glass or metal tube (usually slipped over the fourth or ring finger) along the strings. The pedal steel, which developed from the Hawaiian guitar, is generally associated with country music and uses a sophisticated system of levers and pedals to pull and push notes sharp or flat from the original pitch. The tone is brighter, clearer and generally less gutsy than regular slide guitar.

John Paul Jones takes the first solo on *You Shook Me* on Hammond organ, showing his versatility with a fine piece of playing (the bass guitar in this track is there to underpin rather than to embellish). Plant's blues harp solo is interspersed with moans and whimpers, while Page uses the orgasm technique for his guitar solo again, this time almost certainly on his Telecaster.
Page was concerned at criticism from some quarters which said the debut album owed more than a little to The Jeff Beck Group. *You Shook Me* had appeared on Beck's 'Truth' album and Jeff was more than a little annoyed at the rival version's success. *Dazed And Confused* had been in The Yardbirds' set for some time (as *I'm Confused*) and Beck was bound to have played it live. Of all the tracks on 'Led Zeppelin' this is probably most reminiscent of the way Beck writes and plays. However, Page was incensed at the idea of any such cribbing. Jimmy: "It really pissed me off when people compared our first album to The Jeff Beck Group and said it was very close conceptually. It was utter nonsense. The only similarity was that we'd both come out of The Yardbirds and had both acquired certain riffs individually from The Yardbirds."

As it happens, *Dazed And Confused* could be held up as the blueprint for a particular style of Zeppelin song. It opens with the basic riff played by Jones on his Fender Jazz bass. The high intro 'harmonics' from Page's guitar are treated with a mild wah-wah effect – could this be the same DeArmond pedal used for Dave Berry's *The Crying Game*? The main riff is played by both guitar and bass, an octave apart, before a second octave is added using an overdubbed guitar; the three lines together provide a powerful and unusual sound, aided by the fact that the guitars are played using

MAIN PICTURE

Jimmy and Les Paul Standard: the perfect Page pose.

Jimmy's violin bow technique. The improvised middle section, which includes typical Plant vocalisations and a cooking solo from Page – again, probably the Telecaster with the treble rolled off – shows just how tight the band had become with only a few rehearsals and one short tour. It also hints at what was to come in *Whole Lotta Love* on the subsequent record.
The strains of Jones's swirling Hammond organ usher in side two and *Your Time Is Gonna Come*. While the feel of the Hammond is reminiscent of the intro to Joe Cocker's famous Beatles cover version, the song's acoustic guitar riff – a fairly typical sequence that falls under the fingers in the key of D Major – owes more than a passing nod to the Traffic track *Mr Fantasy*. (It should be noted that musical comparisons are made purely as a point of reference for the reader and do not imply anything untoward on the part of the band!)
Page had long since loved the lyrical guitar playing of the American, Bert Jansch. *Black Mountain Side* was Jimmy's sensitive adaptation of Jansch's *Black Waterside* and a respectful tip of the hat to his hero. Jansch was a master of unusual guitar tunings and Page retuned his guitar in order to perform the number. The Indian tabla drum was played by session musician Viram Jasani. Again, Jimmy probably played Mickie Most's Gibson J200 acoustic.

Communication Breakdown was another raucous rocker. Short but very sweet, the song's verse features a stuttering chord riff of E, D, A, D. The seemingly simple chorus is made subtly more complex by the use of 'pushed' beats and syncopation, plus Jones's inventive extension of the standard rock'n'roll bassline. Page's fiery solo on the Telecaster shows the guitar's more usual attack, Jimmy having left the tone control wide open to create that searing sound. Plant's delivery on this track – and there's the distinction, he *delivered* – included the descending wails and spluttered improvisations which would become trademarks; often copied, rarely equalled, but never bettered.

I Can't Quit You Baby was perhaps the album's only gratuitous outing. Another Willie Dixon blues, this time the bass plods along, with Page's guitar answering Plant's vocals in uninspired, generic style. Hendrix would have done it far better! The guitar solo is messy and repetitious, a far cry from the daring work on *Dazed And Confused* and the machinegun-like accuracy of *Good Times Bad Times*.

'Led Zeppelin' closes with *How Many More Times*, an eight minute, 28 second band workout encompassing mid-tempo, BB King style riffing, a bolero section not unlike Hendrix's *Third Stone From The Sun*, plus bluesy (and uncredited) renditions of *The Hunter* and *Rosie*. The improvisational nature of *How Many More Times* made it a great finisher for the Scandinavian dates. As with *Dazed And Confused*, Page included his legendary violin bowing technique on this track. First persuaded to try the idea by a session violinist some years earlier, he had made something of a party piece of the technique. "It was an extension of what I'd been working on with The Yardbirds," he explained, "although I'd never had that much chance to see how far I could stretch the bowing technique on record." Page and The Creation's guitarist Eddie Phillips both used the violin bow idea in the mid 60s. Some contemporaries state that Phillips did it first, but it's unlikely that one guitarist borrowed the idea from the other or cares particularly about the order of events. During the making of 'Led Zeppelin' the group played a few British dates. The first gig using the new name came in mid October at Surrey University. The following two nights, however, the band worked at The Marquee Club in London and then Liverpool University; the Marquee gig was reviewed with mild enthusiasm by the British music press, while the Liverpool date was notable mainly as the quartet's last ever performance as The New Yardbirds.

PICTURES

Plant: mean, moody, magnificent!

Peter Grant was not lying idle during this period either. The band needed a contract and so Grant flew to New York, a rough mix of the album clutched firmly in his grasp. According to Grant,

the deal had been agreed in principle before the band was even together; apparently it was enough that Page was involved. Of course, The Yardbirds had been signed both in Britain and in the States and it might have seemed logical to suppose that Grant would seek to renegotiate with the band's old record company, Columbia. But never the predictable one, the manager arranged a meeting, not with Columbia but with Jerry Wexler and Ahmet Ertegun at Atlantic. Although famous for its blues, soul and jazz artists, the label had already signed British group Yes and were apparently convinced by UK singer Dusty Springfield of the new band's potential – again, probably because of Page. "Ahmet Ertegun and Jerry Wexler really believed in him," said Grant.

Grant played the consummate brinkman, acting as though his group (in reality still a very unknown quantity) were the hottest property around (he probably also intimated that every other major company was champing at the bit to sign them). "You don't know my price," was his reply to Atlantic's opening gambit, and his daring ploy paid off. He left Wexler and Ertegun with an offer of a five year contract in his pocket, and a deal for a reputed $200,000 (then £50,000) the largest amount yet paid for a new band. Most managers would be more than satisfied with such gains. Not Grant. He also landed the biggest royalty rate ever agreed for a group and, quite unheard of before and rarely since, complete artistic control over every vital aspect of his charges' career.

MAIN PICTURE

Plant: mean, moody, magnificent!

Jimmy flew over to America with the completed master tapes and the deal was signed. Even the ebullient Grant must have been surprised at the success of his visit. And surely noone could have predicted the speed and ferocity with which this latest bunch of lads from England was about to conquer America, and eventually the world.

On November 9th, Robert married his girlfriend Maureen. That evening the band played their first London gig as Led Zeppelin, at The Roundhouse in Chalk Farm. For their services they received the royal sum of £150 (at that time around $600) and a standing ovation. A series of London club dates saw the group through most of what remained of 1968. But England seemed not quite ready to accept the quartet that was soon to dominate the world's stadium stages.

The first concert on American soil was scheduled for Boxing Day, in Denver Colorado, supporting acid rock band Vanilla Fudge. Page was the only one of the four to have visited the States previously, so it was new experience time again for Plant, Jones and Bonham. They flew out on Christmas Eve, Grant having given express instructions to the band to "blast them out". And blast them out they certainly did.

American fans went wild for the new music. The so called 'British Invasion' of The Beatles, Stones, Hollies, Herman's Hermits and any other shaggy haired group of relatively talented young individuals, had had a profound effect on America. But when Zeppelin played their first US dates they became aware of two further advantages: not only was their musicianship outstanding, but they were

also a particularly attractive bunch of young men. The girls loved Plant's flowing blond hair, his good looks and unrestrained sexual presence. Page, the classically handsome Englishman among the quartet, was idolised by aspiring guitarists and adoring females alike, while Jones and Bonham gained their own fair share of admirers on both fronts.

Grant's experience in handling American tours was extensive. "I had been going to the States since 1964 when I went with The Animals," he stated. "By the time I got Zeppelin I knew America inside out. I knew Bill Graham, for example, and knew that if you got his two Fillmores (East and West), the Boston Tea Party and Detroit, they were the most important places for the group." The tour was arranged through top promoters Premier Talent, who ensured the highest possible profile for Led Zeppelin at all times. Cities were chosen precisely for this reason, and The Yardbirds' previous West Coast success was capitalised upon to great effect. Pre-release copies of the new album were sent to influential DJs at leading radio stations, and by January 17th, when the record was officially delivered to a well primed public, advance sales stood in excess of 50,000.

But the publicity which garnered so much public interest in the band had the effect of working against them, as far as the press were concerned. Perhaps expecting a finely honed, flawlessly executed and perfectly produced package, the music critics were less than ecstatic, levelling accusations of sloppiness towards the album. According to some, Zeppelin were also greedy, prefabricated and hyped. It seemed they couldn't win. Page retaliated: "Before they saw us in

America there was a blast of publicity and they heard all about the money being advanced by the record company. So the reaction was, 'Ah, capitalist group'. They realised we weren't when they saw us playing a three hour, non stop show every night." As for the alleged propaganda (ignoring for a moment the name of Zep's publishing company, Superhype), Page commented: "For anyone to imply that Led Zeppelin were prefabricated or hyped upon a gullible public is grossly unfair." The fans still went wild and the tour was an unqualified success, the band members perhaps seeing for the first time their potential for world domination.

The American tour was spent in support of major US acts of the time, such as Country Joe and the Fish and Iron Butterfly. Neither band was a match for the onslaught that was Zeppelin. In fact, at New York's Fillmore East on February 1st and 2nd, just before they flew back to England, the group left Iron Butterfly feeling like bridesmaids at their own wedding. Zeppelin themselves were unsure as to why they made it so big so soon. Page: "I can only think that we were aware of dynamics at a time when everyone else was into that drawn out, West Coast style of playing." But Jimmy knew the exact moment when they broke through: "San Francisco. There were other gigs, like the Boston Tea Party and the Kinetic Circus in Chicago, but after the San Francisco gig it was just – bang!"

PICTURES

Out On The Tiles!

Meanwhile, 'Led Zeppelin' was ascending the charts apace, fuelling interest in the gigs which in turn created further record sales. Eventually peaking at No 10 the album stayed on the charts for an unbroken 73 weeks.

In early March the band returned to Britain from what was a killer US tour by anyone's standards. But where The Beatles had come down the gangway to hordes of adoring press and cheering public, Led Zeppelin received no such welcome. Despite their Top 10 American success, a small club tour (at between £60 and £140 per night!) was all the group could look forward to on home soil. During the tour 'Led Zeppelin' received some UK airplay and news of the American success began filtering through. The album was eventually released on March 28th and made No 6 on the British chart, where it eventually spent a total of 79 weeks. Led Zeppelin had come home – and Plant had made it by age 20.

'Led Zeppelin II' The Big Time

If Led Zeppelin received regular criticism over the years and throughout the albums it was from a hardcore following that had been turned on by the band's own invention, rock, and didn't really want to know about the other stuff. Acoustic epics and ethnic forays were not for them. They needed heavy riffs, searing solos, screaming vocals and a drum sound that could raise Beelzebub.

'Led Zeppelin II' would probably characterise classic Zep for fans and casual followers alike. Where the debut offering had been a quick dip into a studio to record what was essentially the band's new live set, the second album showed deliberation, experimentation and above all the group's individual personalities beginning to make their presence felt through the music. Listen to the strength and inventiveness of the bass playing of John Paul Jones on every track; the power, tightness and flair of Bonzo's drumming; the sophistication that had so quickly developed in Plant's voice; and the sheer creative brilliance of Page on every front.

Unlike 'Led Zeppelin', which encompassed a total of 15 days' work, the follow up was recorded in various studios in London, New York and Los Angeles, between May and September 1969. The band's schedule had become somewhat hectic and recording had to be fitted in around the daily grind of touring. The first album was still in the charts in most of the group's territories and so Zeppelin found themselves promoting old material while writing and recording new songs. As Page wearily explained at the time: "We've been so busy that we just weren't able to go into one studio and polish the album off. We'd put a rhythm track down in London, add the voice in New York, overdub harmonica in Vancouver and then come back to New York."

MAIN PICTURE

Heartbreaker!

On the first record, songwriting credits were limited to 'Trad, arr Page', various blues artists and a few Page, Jones, Bonham compositions. This was in the main due to Plant's earlier signing with CBS preventing him from being involved. The credits on 'Led Zeppelin II' would read very differently, with Jimmy and Robert collaborating on no fewer than five tracks; the rest (with the exception of the instrumental *Moby Dick*, to which Plant did not contribute) being band compositions.

But Robert was becoming a good lyricist. He took his songwriting very seriously indeed, always searching for meaningful topics and the perfect way of saying what he wanted to say. As he put it at the time: "What I want is to sit down and write songs and say to the rest of the band, 'Listen to this'."

After the March club tour of the UK came a second Scandinavian jaunt (including one 30 minute TV

show which was to be seen in the UK a staggering 20 years later!). There were also several more gigs at home. On March 21st the band made their only ever live British TV performance; *Communication Breakdown* was the number chosen for BBC2's How Late It Is. Two days later Zeppelin played a session for John Peel's Top Gear show on BBC Radio One. For many British teenagers it was this airing of the band that would spark off a life long love affair with Led Zeppelin and with rock music in general.

On March 25th, Page Plant, Jones and Bonzo performed for the much hyped 'Super Session'. This was a filmed get together of some unlikely playing partners, including Eric Clapton, The Modern Jazz Quartet, Stephen Stills, Buddy Miles, Roland Kirk, Jon Hiseman's Colosseum and Buddy Guy. The idea was to put musicians from entirely different backgrounds together and watch the results. Some of the jazzers were dismissive of the rock element, some of whom had trouble with the complex chords and changes found in modern jazz. In the end the film had trouble finding distribution, but it was nevertheless an interesting exercise and the inclusion of Zeppelin as the hard rock element showed that the new genre had truly arrived.

As 'Led Zeppelin' was finally released in the UK (March 28th) the band played a few more British dates before it was back to the USA in April for their first headlining tour. This time Zep would command four times the fee paid for the first American outing. The tour opened at the Fillmore West on April 24th. Julie Driscoll and The Brian Augur Trinity (No 1 hit *This Wheel's On Fire*) were the band's support for much of the tour and the British broadside stormed America.

It was on this tour that Zeppelin made their big hit with the girls. Last time they had been a handsome bunch of English lads; now they had an album in the Top 10 and were stars. Throughout the band's career they would be acclaimed as the group who partied above and beyond the call of duty. But with their customary secrecy, elusiveness and the protection of the omniscient Mr Grant, the stories remain, by and large, heresay.

Plant was amazed to find himself hailed as an object of lust. "I've been told I'm a sexual beacon," he said. "It seems funny that a few months ago I was an ungratified singer and now they're calling me the next sex symbol." Robert's reasoning for why he was singled out in this way was pragmatic, if a little blunt: "Maybe if they can see a cock through a pair of trousers, then that must make you a sex symbol," he shrugged. "Since I'm the only one who doesn't have a guitar or drums in front of mine, I suppose I started out with more of a chance than anyone else in the band."

After the headline US tour, during which the band's debut album had been flying high in the *Billboard* Top 10, the weary quartet returned home to the odd gig and radio session. June 13th saw the start of the first UK tour proper, commencing at Birmingham Town Hall and including the Playhouse Theatre in London (the show was taped for BBC2's In Concert series), the Bath open air festival and culminating in two shows at the Royal Albert Hall.

In July it was back to the States once more, and although the reception the group was receiving everywhere was nothing short of fantastic, an element of weariness was already setting in. They wanted to get back to wives, friends and families. Bonham: "There are times when you sit down and say, 'I wanna go home'. It's not the playing – I could do that all day. It's just the being away that gets you down sometimes. I still enjoy going through towns we haven't been to before, but you get fed up with places like New York, because they're not interesting any more."

Plant was more specific about his desire to get back: "Tours are exhausting, no doubt about that. The thing is, that when you step off the plane at Heathrow, all the exhaustion lifts. I suppose America isn't bad, but it just isn't home. You can be tired and overworked every day at home, but it's okay because it *is* home. That's the difference."

During this American tour the band played the Newport Jazz Festival and were originally to have appeared at the legendary Woodstock, but that was not to be. One can only wonder at the effect that an appearance by Zeppelin would have had at the event. At it was, Woodstock was dominated by the British, with acts such as Joe Cocker, The Who and Ten Years After going down a storm, and honorary Brit, Jimi Hendrix (America hadn't wanted to know him) stealing the show. The tour ended at the Texas International Festival in Dallas and the Zeppelins came home for a deserved break. Page went to Morocco, where he submerged himself in the local music. Here the first seeds were perhaps sewn for the stunning *Kashmir*, which would not appear until the sixth album, 'Physical Grafitti'.

'Led Zeppelin II' was completed in September of 1969 and released on 31st October.

If Zeppelin could be summed up musically in five letters, those letters would be B D B D E, the opening notes of the second album and the basis for the most gloriously simple rock riff ever devised: *Whole Lotta Love*. Critics have tried to describe this epic with varying degrees of success. But the sheer excitement and power of the track defies all the superlatives.

Musically it's the most basic of ideas; just three notes of the Pentatonic scale. But it's what Page and the band did with those three notes that makes it unique: the way the initial riff builds using layered guitars, Jones doubling the line on bass; Plant's blatantly sexual lyrics and Bonzo's tommy gun drum fill into the chorus, with Page's sneering slide guitar adding an extra slice of spite. Like the band itself, the song was definitely greater than the sum of its parts.

Jimmy was now using his old Gibson Les Paul Standard, a much beefier sounding guitar than the Telecaster and the instrument with which he would become most associated.

Whole Lotta Love's brilliantly assembled middle section is simply the sex act set to music. The album was mixed with the help of Eddie Kramer, an engineer who had been heavily involved with Jimi Hendrix's recorded work. Hendrix was a master of the new stereo recording techniques and used every trick in the book to create aural magic. Page and Kramer worked together at New York's A&R Studios to perfect a piece that would out-Hendrix Hendrix.

MAIN PICTURE

Led Zeppelin! No smoke without fire?

RIGHT PICTURE

Jones with Alembic bass.

The two minute foray starts with Bonzo on hi-hat, ride cymbals and overdubbed bongos. Then Page begins the mayhem. Taking the slide guitar concept to extremes, Jimmy summons the weirdest of noises from his instrument as he pans the tracks to and fro across the stereo spectrum, building in intensity from growls to whoops and then wails, all the while duelling with Plant's blatant vocalisations. Bonzo almost brings the sequence to a premature climax with his first drum fill, but he's only teasing. More of everything, then the real orgasm: a brutal Bonham assault and then Jimmy launches into one of the most exciting electric guitar solos ever committed to record. The song finishes with

Robert in outrageous form. It was probably his "Keep a-coolin' baby" and the impossibly high screams, drenched in echo by Page and Kramer, which incited a thousand pretenders to bid for his throne. None would ever come close to unseating the champion.

Plant later emphasised how important this number was for him and the band. *"Whole Lotta Love* is something that I personally need," explained the singer, "something I just have to have. We bottle it all up, and when we go on stage we can let it all pour out. I suppose in a way it's become a Zeppelin cliché, but it's also a vehicle to other things. The song is very good for us."

The fantastic middle section was edited out of the version of the song when it was released as an American single (it made the Top 5 in the States and hit the No 1 spot in certain European countries). But Grant's policy was that no singles were to be released in Great Britain. And the band's contract with Atlantic gave them complete artistic control over their product. So although the label were all set to repeat their heroes' US single success in the UK, it was never to be.

Some of the lyrics in *Whole Lotta Love* were borrowed from *You Need Love* by bluesman Willie Dixon. Dixon was not credited on the record and Zeppelin received their first writ for plagiarism. The case never made it to trial, however, all parties being happy to settle out of court.

If *Whole Lotta Love* was a distillation of the band's basic, instinctive or carnal nature, then the next track on 'II', *What Is And What Should Never Be* represented the cerebral side of Led Zeppelin. It was also chock full of ideas from the whole group and could easily be held up as the archetypal heavy rock ballad. Like so much that Zeppelin was to create, instigate or invent, it would be copied by almost every rock group since, but like a pack of greyhounds after a mechanical hare, the outcome of the chase would be a foregone conclusion every time.

ALL PICTURES & OVERLEAF

The many poses of Page!

The track switches from style to style, beginning with Plant's flanged vocal line, "And if I say to you tomorrow." Flanging is the use of two identical sounds with one slowed down and put slightly out of tune with another; it creates a dreamy effect and is perhaps best remembered on The Small Faces' *Itchycoo Park*. The term 'flanging' has been credited to John Lennon, who liked to press his hand against the central flange of a turning spool of tape to slow it down.

Page's strummed electric guitar, using A7add6 and E7add9 chords, and Plant's unusually soft vocal set up a deceptively gentle feel to the song. Jones's bass is at its best here; punctuating the simplicity with smooth melodic lines. As so often was to be the case, Bonham's powerful snare shots break the calm and lead into the tune's devastating riff. The solo is typical of Page in that it's *not* typical . Played on slide guitar, it comes as a fresh melody out of the blue, sweetly at first but more insistent as it progresses into the song's heavy section.

It's worth noting that Page's guitar sounds – and he employed as wide a range of tones as anyone – were rarely as overdriven or distorted as those of today's players. Jimmy's use of cleaner settings required more accuracy in both picking and fretting (distortion softens the sound and can smooth out playing deficiencies) and went a long way towards providing the real power in the Zeppelin sound.

Track three, *The Lemon Song,* saw Zeppelin in trouble with the copyright laws again. The song was originally credited on the album sleeve as a band composition. But the track bore too striking a resemblance to the classic blues *Killing Floor* for the original composer's liking (Robert's exhortation to "squeeze my lemon till the juice runs down my leg" notwithstanding!). In reality a combination of several blues numbers that the group had been playing live (or to which Plant had been spontaneously inserting old blues lyrics), *The Lemon Song* was duly re-credited to Chester Burnett and publishers Jewel Music. Some pre-recorded cassettes even carried the *Killing Floor* title.

The Lemon Song is more or less a straight band 'take' using the basic three musician lineup. During Jimmy's first superb solo flight his Les Paul's second string slips badly flat, but with Zeppelin a good take meant more than individual perfection (electronic tuners were not widely available until later, so it was actually not uncommon for musicians to be out of tune with themselves or each other).

Thank You is Robert's touching ode to his wife Maureen. It features a mature vocal from Plant and some dynamic Hammond organ work from John Paul – in fact the song was often used as a live showcase for Jones's keyboard talents. Here Jimmy plays an electric 12 string guitar, at the time more readily associated with the West Coast sound of The Byrds' *Mr Tambourine Man*, or The Beatles' *A Hard Day's Night* than heavy rock. His acoustic guitar solo seems uninventive and lacklustre by his usual high standards.

Plant's self confessed love of West Coast music is also clearly audible on *Thank You*, especially in the harmony vocal sections. It must be remembered that Zeppelin were writing their new album while on tour. They were often in the States and regularly in the musical company of West Coast acts such as The Doors and Iron Butterfly (who were usually made to look weak by comparison), so it is not surprising to find such a range of influences on the new record.

Heartbreaker, recorded at A&R Studios in New York, is based around another classic Zeppelin riff and tells the story of another big bad girl. This track was Jimmy's platform for a display of digital dexterity virtually unheard of at the time. The song's riff section stops abruptly and Page adopts the orgasm technique once more (the initial spluttering and repeated lick was used for a BBC Radio One rock show theme tune). Jimmy then launches into a one man and his guitar demolition derby, cramming hundreds of notes (not all of them cleanly executed, it has to be said) into less than a minute and setting a million young guitarists on a trek for their musical holy grail.

The song's third distinct section has Jimmy ruling the roost again. A big chordal riff in A leads into what is arguably the best guitar solo on the album; it bubbles up through the chords until Page finds himself on the top strings, bending, slurring and hammering notes; pushing the timing, flailing with his pick and skating on the very brink of his technique. Bonham and Jones seem happy to adopt supporting roles and even Plant is content to sing in unruffled and easy fashion.

Reputedly written about a West Coast groupie, *Livin' Lovin' Maid (She's Just A Woman)*, has Page return to the Fender Telecaster (hear its more incisive tone). Essentially a mid tempo head banger, the number sees Jones creating some impressively melodic bass lines and Bonzo playing as funkily as you like. Harmony vocals and a short but sweet guitar break helped make the song radio friendly. Originally *Whole Lotta Love*'s American B-side, the song was eventually re-released as the A-side and made a respectable No 65 on the *Billboard* chart. *She's Just A Woman* was never popular with the band and they apparently never played it live.

"With things like *Ramble On* we were definitely deviating from the original Zeppelin intensity, but without losing quality" said Plant of the number that starts on acoustic guitar before building into an intense and riffy chorus. Jimmy again retuned his acoustic guitar and supplied a very Stephen Stills-like backing for Plant's sensitive vocal. Robert perhaps meant Stills when he said: "I think the open chord sort of thing, like Neil Young also uses, is beautiful. I'm obsessed with that type of music, particularly when it has really good, intense lyrics."

Throughout 'Led Zeppelin II' the interaction between the musicians is quite amazing. Yes, they were seasoned players and established touring musicians, but still only in their early twenties. On their second record they played as though they'd been together ten years, not just ten months. Bonham's fantastic snare and bass drum work and the way he syncopates against the basic rhythm may escape the casual listener, as could Jones's tuneful inventions on the bass. Page is often thought of as Mr Lead Guitar, but his rhythm work is so often the binding agent in a delicately balanced recipe.

Moby Dick is Cockney rhyming slang for 'sick' – as in throwing up. Originally played as early as the first US tour, the instrumental was originally titled *Pat's Delight* after Bonham's wife and was subsequently adopted for use as BBC2 TV's Disco 2 theme tune. Another devastatingly simple riff doubled by bass and guitar, the tune was in fact the drummer's live showcase from the start. Whether drum solos ever work on record or not is for the individual to decide. Bonzo certainly loved playing the track live and in later years the number developed into a 20 minute extravaganza. But for many the highlight of track three, side two of 'Led Zeppelin II' was, again, Page's guitar solo, which leapt out of the number like an uncoiling spring and showed his unerring ability to surprise and excite the listener.

The album's final track, *Bring It On Home* opens with Page playing boogie woogie rhythm guitar to Plant's harp and vocal parody of a Memphis bluesman. It fires up into a powerful riff, sometimes harmonised by Page on overdubbed guitar. But essentially *Bring It On Home* is a one chord, blues-funk filler, the highlight of which is Bonham's obvious enjoyment at the kit.
Due to the album proving so difficult to write and record, Plant and Page were worried that perhaps it had been overdone. They were so close to the project that the work seemed interminable and the songs were sounding old and stale before they'd even been released. As Jimmy said at the time: "I do worry that the second album is turning out so differently from the first. We may have

overstepped the mark, but there again there are enough Led Zeppelin trademarks in there. It's hard rock, no doubt about that." Plant was more positive: "No matter what the critics said, the proof of the pudding was that it got a lot of people off. As far as I was concerned it was a good, maybe even great road album."

Released in late October 1969, the album's sales were spectacular. It made No 1 in the UK and stayed on the chart for 138 weeks.

Led Zeppelin were to undertake one more US tour in 1969 and it began with a momentous gig at the prestigious Carnegie Hall in New York, home of classical music in America and a venue for the major jazz names. As the first rock band ever to play the famous hall it was a big night for the group, especially Bonham, whose heroes Gene Krupa and Buddy Rich had both sat on the same stage.

The fourth US tour that year finished at San Francisco's Winterland ballroom. Four weary but very rich and extremely famous young men came home to receive gold and platinum discs to honour sales of their first record (after the reception Page went to Berkeley Square to buy himself a Rolls Royce). But tracks for the next album had already been tried out. One was a slow blues called *Since I've Been Lovin' You*.

TOP PICTURE

Friends.

LEFT PICTURE

Dazed And Confused!

'Led Zeppelin III' Acoustic Alchemy

Jimmy Page had dominated the first two albums. Not only had he produced them but his songwriting and certainly his musical influence was the greatest by far. Of course that was hardly surprising, since at the outset Jimmy was the experienced one (whilst Jones was a master of the studio, unlike Page he had not travelled the globe as a member of a top band). So although Jimmy had led the others into the world they now occupied, each band member now had star status and each one wanted, and deserved, a say in what went on.

Two potential tracks for the third album had already been recorded in November 69. *Since I've Been Loving You* and *Jennings Farm Blues* were both tried out at Olympic; the latter found its way onto the record as the acoustic *Bron-Y-Aur Stomp.*

Plant wanted to get away from the jet set life that he and the others had been living for the past eighteen months. Especially he wanted no repeat of the making of the last record, which had been put together under virtually impossible conditions. Robert remembered a cottage in the Welsh countryside where he had stayed as a youngster. "He was going on about what a beautiful place it was," recalled Page, "and I became keen to go there. So off we went, taking along our guitars of course. It wasn't a case of 'Let's go and knock off a few songs in the country', it was more a case of wanting to get away for a bit and have a good time."

MAIN PICTURE

Rock And Roll!

The cottage, called Bron-Y-Aur (hence the *Stomp!*) and situated on the side of a hill in Snowdonia, was to be a source of much inspiration for the new album. But 'Led Zeppelin III', the most eagerly awaited release of 1970 and back ordered by hundreds of thousands by the time it reached the shops, was to be received with mixed feelings. Fans expecting the same leap in power and tightness that characterised albums one and two were to be disappointed; those who loved the breadth and diversity in the band's music would appreciate the considerable effort that had been put into 'III'; new Led Zeppelin acolytes would call it their greatest work and cite the earlier efforts as unsubtle by comparison.

Zeppelin were now the biggest band in the world and one of the hardest working. They would break every kind of concert attendance record, including The Beatles' famous Shea Stadium gig in 1965, where 55,000 fans had gathered in awe of their heroes (at Tampa Stadium Florida in 1973, a crowd of 56,800 would amass to greet its own fab four!).

Zeps 'I' and 'II' were selling in bucketloads and the band were all millionaires, prone to the usual excesses of young men with money. Cars were a great source of interest and Bonham, in particular, loved to collect them; he was known to walk into a dealer with a briefcase full of cash to pay for his latest dream machine.

But there was also a sensible side to the group's spending. They all bought property; houses and farms, usually secluded and treated as a refuge from the glare of the spotlight and the pace of touring. "They say the village folk never die, they have to be shot," said Plant of his life in the country. "I just revel in those country things; chickens, goats and my horse. After reading Tolkein I just had to have a place in the country."

The year of 'Led Zeppelin III' began with a week long British tour, kicking off in Birmingham on January 7th but hitting a minor problem when Robert was slightly hurt in a road accident; the group's Edinburgh date had to be cancelled. That same month, *Whole Lotta Love* reached No 4 on America's *Billboard* chart. In February the band headed to Copenhagen to start a European tour which ended three weeks later at the Montreux Jazz Festival. A week off and then it was back once more across the Atlantic, beginning their fifth tour of North America in Vancouver, Canada.

At this time the police forces of certain American cities were becoming notorious for their behaviour at concerts. It was not uncommon for groups of officers to instigate violence among the crowds and even to intimidate the bands they were supposedly there to protect. As the greatest group on the circuit – and no doubt occasionally as 'long haired Limey faggots' – Led Zeppelin received their fair share of abuse. But when touring the Southern states they were also easy prey for some of the more aggressive types who inhabited the roadhouses and truckstops. Bonham: "The restaurant scene in the South can be unbelievable. We've stopped for a coffee and watched everybody else in the place get service; people who came in after us. Everybody sits and glares at you, waiting and hoping that you'll explode and a scene will start."

The group even had a gun pulled on them in Texas. Bonzo: "Some guy was shouting out and giving us general crap about our hair, so we simply gave it back to him. We were leaving after the show and this same guy turned up at the door. He pulls out this gun and says, 'You guys gonna do any shouting now?' We cleared out of there tout de suite!"

Back at Bron-Y-Aur Plant and Page were getting off on the tranquillity of it all. They took along a couple of roadies and spent the evenings sat around log fires, "With pokers being plunged into cider and that sort of thing," recounted Page. "As the nights

RIGHT PICTURE

"Down By The Seaside"

wore on, the guitars came out and numbers were being written. It wasn't really planned as a working holiday but some songs did come out of it."

The numbers that Page and Plant were to compose at Bron-Y-Aur – which carried none of the modern amenities such as electricity, hot water etc – were of an understandably organic and acoustic nature, leading some critics to accuse the group of copying bands like Crosby Stills and Nash. Page griped at the comparison: "That LP had just come out and because acoustic guitars had come to the forefront, all of a sudden it was 'Led Zeppelin go acoustic'."

The turning inner wheel theme for the original gatefold record sleeve went slightly wrong. Intended by Page to mimick crop rotation charts or, as he later put it, "garden calendars or those zoo wheel things that tell you when to plant cauliflowers or how long whales are pregnant," the design looked whimsical and trite. Apparently the artist, Richard Drew, had not been correctly briefed for the commission and the album's deadline meant an inevitable and embarrassing compromise. Jimmy described it as "teeny-boppish."

The organic theme continued as the group began rehearsing the new numbers at Headley Grange, a rambling old Hampshire manor house. Much of the album would be recorded here, using The Rolling Stones' mobile studio. Other sessions would take place at their old haunt Olympic, with some extra work carried out at Chris Blackwell's new Island

studios. Final mixing was completed in Ardent studios Memphis, during the band's US tour in August – their sixth.

Of course, not all the music on 'III' was to be acoustic. The album opens with the intense *Immigrant Song*, a wailing war cry inspired by Zeppelin's trip to Reykjavik in Iceland. Plant was put out by criticism of the 'pomposity' of his lyric – 'I am a Viking from the land of ice and snow'. "We weren't being pompous," he retaliated. "We did come from the land of ice and snow; we were guests of the Icelandic Government on a cultural mission. We were invited to play a concert in Reykjavik and the day before we arrived all the civil servants went on strike and the gig was going to be cancelled. The university prepared a concert hall for us to play in and it was phenomenal. The response we had from the kids was remarkable and we had a great time. *Immigrant Song* was about that trip and it was the opening track of an album that was intended to be incredibly different."

Immigrant Song was based around a simple octave riff in the key of F sharp. Pompous or not, Plant excelled, his vocal cords more elastic than ever – the touring was paying off.

MAIN PICTURES

Jones adapted a new hairstyle for each tour, to maintain his anonymity.

Friends was a Page/Plant composition, conceived in Wales and containing elements of Jimmy's folk and Eastern influences. Its hypnotic nature only comes across after several hearings; a casual listen – something which record reviewers know all too much about – reveals only a pleasant but indifferent offering.

The intro to the third track *Celebration Day* was cleverly linked to the outro of *Friends* using a Moog synthesiser. This was due to the master tape somehow becoming damaged at that point. Here is Zeppelin in funk rock mode. Jones harks back to his Motown influences and Page employs a classic rhythm guitar lick and some bluesy slide guitar fills; there's no let up for Bonzo's Paiste cymbals and, again, Plant's range seems limitless. A fine solo from Jimmy, sounding more worked out than his usual 'head down and go for it' forays of the previous albums.

For many the highlight on 'Led Zeppelin III' is the slow blues *Since I've Been Loving You*. Jones played organ and bass pedals, temporarily putting aside his 1961 Fender Jazz bass to create those resonant and sustaining bottom notes. Page's guitar intro owes much to that great English blues guitarist Peter Green, late of John Mayall's Bluesbreakers and founder member of Fleetwood

Mac. Jimmy's gentle then spiteful touch created much of the dynamics for the song. Plant is on top form here, spitting out the lyrics and holding on to those high notes with consummate ease, while there's a wonderful irony in Bonham's brutal drum assault on such a gentle piece.

Page's solo bursts in, ignoring the convention that says blues guitar breaks start slowly and build to a crescendo (the thinking there is that if all the aces are played in the first few seconds, the guitarist has nowhere to go; effectively he has trumped himself). Page, of course, always kept an ace or two up his sleeve and consequently the solo is full of peaks, troughs and climaxes. At times Jimmy plays notes which are not strictly correct, although as usual the performance ruled over such minor considerations and the solo stands as one of the most dramatic in all of rock.

Out On The Tiles, with Bonham's manic drumming and Page and Jones's insistent riff, marked a link between tracks like *Heartbreaker* and *Moby Dick* from 'Led Zeppelin II' and *Black Dog* from the forthcoming record. Never seen as a classic Zep track, the song still has a great feel and shows the often neglected funkiness in the band's output – mainly due to Bonham, who certainly inspired this track with one of his drum riffs and was the instigator of many others.

On *Gallows Pole*, an old Leadbelly folk tune, Jones played mandolin and bass while Jimmy added six and 12 string guitars and banjo. Page took an early 12 string guitar arrangement as the basis for the Zeppelin version. Jimmy: "I first heard it on an old Folkways LP by Fred Gerlach, a 12 string player who was, I believe, the first white to play the instrument. I used his version as a basis and completely changed the arrangement." Within the stomping, folksy feel of the track Page's electric guitar sounds more like violin.

Plant justified the unpopularity of the acoustic or folk influenced feel of many tracks on 'Led Zeppelin III' like this: "You see, here I am, the lead singer with Led Zeppelin, and underneath I still enjoy Fairport Convention and Buffalo Springfield. Some people may find that surprising, but to tell the truth I've always wanted to go into the realm of that sort of music to a certain degree, without losing the original Zeppelin thing. I don't think we'll go into a decline just because we've got into some different things."

If the rock fans didn't like 'Led Folk', then the country feel of *Tangerine* with its deliberate West Coast influence, Plant's harmony vocals and Jimmy's cheesy pedal steel guitar, might have put them off completely. But if they'd listened more closely they might have heard strains of their beloved *Stairway...* in the chords and arrangement. The Page composition (written during his Yardbirds days) is 'salvaged' some might say by a gorgeous slide guitar solo. But, as Page was to point out to

those who expected the predictable from their heroes, "How they should approach our albums is to forget they ever heard of a band called Led Zeppelin, forget about what they expect to hear and just listen to what's on that particular record."

The modally tuned acoustic guitars on *That's The Way* provided a warm and atmospheric base for Plant's sensitive lyrics and understated vocal. Page plays pedal steel guitar drenched in reverberation but the track manages to retain a rock ballad, rather than an overtly country or folk feel. Had *That's The Way* not been submerged in an album full of folk songs and throwaway ditties it would probably be hailed as one of the band's finest tracks.

If numbers like *Gallows Pole* and *Tangerine* had unnerved those who listened to 'Led Zeppelin III' expecting *Dazed And Confused Part 2* or *Whole Lotta Love Revisited*, the album's final two cuts would seal its fate in the popularity stakes. *Bron-Y-Aur Stomp* and *Hats Off To (Roy) Harper* – while both ably performed and showing Plant's and Page's genuine musical influences – were too easy and throwaway for a band that had put together the brilliant *Ramble On* and the epic *Heartbreaker*. Fans didn't think they'd got their money's worth and, whether Page, Plant and co cared to publicly

ABOVE PICTURE

"Tell me Robert; is it true that Led Zeppelin are splitting up?"

LEFT PICTURE

With his blond flowing locks and his boyish charm, Plant could hardly fail to attract the ladies.

admit it or not, the public's response to 'III' was to shock Zeppelin into action.

On June 28th came one of the band's milestone gigs. They topped the bill at the prestigious Bath Festival in the English West Country, playing to 200,000 British fans who had not really seen the band in this, their natural element. Jimmy wore a yokel's hat and a knee length overcoat! The audience saw the debut of *Kashmir* and were stunned by an early live version of *Since I've Been Loving You*, both from the unfinished new record. Following this came a short tour of Germany, where the group visited the Berlin wall and Plant was unnerved to discover that the city was surrounded on all sides by the then Communist East Germany!

In August the band's sixth US tour commenced in Cincinatti. During this visit Page was to complete the mixing of 'Led Zeppelin III' at Ardent Studios in Memphis (a town which earlier that year had made honorary citizens of the foursome). The tour came to a close at New York's Madison Square Garden on September 19th and the group prepared to head
for home again. They arrived to find they had toppled The Beatles as *Melody Maker*'s best group. They also received more gold discs and were congratulated by the Parliamentary Secretary of the Board of Trade on their outstanding contribution to British exports.

Then came a much needed break, and as 'Led Zeppelin III' hit the streets the band entered Island studios to begin work on their fourth album. It was to be a very different offering indeed.

'Led Zeppelin IV' A Long Time Since The Rock'N' Roll

Although its calibre as a recorded work – in particular Page's superb production – went without question, the fact remained that 'Led Zeppelin III' received a critical pasting. And while the album made the No 1 slot on both sides of the Atlantic, it also proved to be the group's least selling record thus far.

Musically the next outing was to hark back to the power and musical glory that marked 'Led Zeppelin II' as a classic. Never ones to follow protocol, however, Zeppelin decided to play down the record's release, to understate their personalities and even deny the band's name. So it was that the nameless album came to be.

"The words Led Zeppelin do not appear anywhere on this cover," explained Page about the wholly pictorial record sleeve. "And all the other usual credits are missing too. The record company told us we were committing professional suicide, but we said we just wanted to rely on the music." Whether this is four famous young men taking themselves a little too seriously or not, the impact of the new cover was to be powerful. Each member chose a visual symbol to represent himself and consequently (as a result of having to call it *something*) the record has become known as 'Four Symbols', 'Led Zeppelin IV' and 'Untitled', among other less obvious names. We shall refer to it as 'Led Zeppelin IV'.

MAIN PICTURE

Bonzo and the massive Paiste gang that invariably accompanied him on stage.

"My symbol was drawn from sacred symbols of the ancient Mu civilisation," revealed Plant. "It existed about 15,000 years ago as part of a lost continent somewhere in the Pacific ocean, between China and Mexico. The Chinese say these people came from the east and the Mexicans say they came from the west. My symbol does have a further meaning and all I can suggest is that people look it up in a suitable reference work." John Paul Jones chose a runic reference, representing confidence and competence – "because it was difficult to draw" explained Page – while, also according to Jimmy, Bonzo selected his from the same book because he liked its appearance. Plant's explanation of the Bonzo rune goes a little deeper: "I suppose it's the trilogy – man, woman and child – although in Pittsburgh we observed that it was also the emblen of Ballantine beer!"

Page, whose known interest in the occult was to fascinate and concern friends and fans alike, created a design of his own. Looking for all the world like an approximation of the word 'Zoso' (some people also refer to the album by this name) the origins of the Page rune remain elusive, although Robert tells how Jimmy once revealed its

secret to him: "Pagey took me aside and said, 'Look, I'm going to tell you the meaning of this once, and then I shan't ever mention it again'. Would you believe I've now forgotten what it was and Pagey won't tell me. If I know him it'll turn up in some long lost book."

The dawning of 1971 saw the band taking The Stones' mobile studio back to Headley Grange to begin work on the next project in earnest. Recorded during January and February of that year (the tracks were mixed at Olympic in London and Sunset Sound in Los Angeles), the fourth album was to prove to everyone that Zep had lost nothing of their power and creativity. The record contained many of the band's most powerful numbers and, like Zeps 'I' and 'II', the gentler tracks were set perfectly within the context of something much heavier. This allowed them to stand out, rather than be buried beneath more of the same.
In the middle of February the British pop paper *Disc And Music Echo* presented Zeppelin with their World's Top Band' award. The following month the foursome commenced a tour of the UK beginning at Belfast's Ulster Hall. This concert was most notable for the fact that here was to be the first airing of a song not yet released. It would be the standout track on 'Led Zeppelin IV' and was destined to become the most requested tune on American FM radio. The song, of course, was *Stairway To Heaven*.

As if to crush any suspicion that 'IV' would be another jaunty folk foray, the band began the record with one of their meatiest and most convoluted Jones/Page riffs. *Black Dog* was named after an unnamed canine companion which hung around Headley Grange during the album's recording. The riff was inspired by a Muddy Waters blues track that Jones had heard on the album 'Electric Mud'. John Paul liked the way the riff intertwined around itself and kept turning corners, and he wanted to create something similar. "But it couldn't be too simple," insisted the bassist. "I wanted it to turn around on itself. I showed the guys and we fell into it." During rehearsals Bonzo became exasperated with the apparently impossible timing at the end of the riff, the 'turnaround', throwing his sticks in the air and refusing to play. But it came together when the

drummer realised that he simply had to count in normal 4/4 timing – "as if there was *no*

PICTURES

Bonham: triumph and turmoil.

turnaround," explained Jones.

Page's arrangement of *Black Dog*, with its lone vocal and answering heavy riff was inspired by Fleetwood Mac's hit single *Oh Well*, which adopted a very similar ploy. Jimmy's playout solo uses four separate tracks of guitar and, apart from the Leslie effect riff at the beginning and end, is rather disappointing; not only does it sound stilted and inarticulate by normal Page standards, but the timing is suspect and Jimmy's Les Paul has slipped flat of pitch with the rest of the band.

Rock And Roll came about as Bonham broke off from what the group was playing and went unexpectedly into an old Little Richard number. Page: "It was a spontaneous combustion. We were doing something else at the time, but Bonzo played the beginning of *Good Golly Miss Molly* with the tape still running, and I just started doing that part of the riff." The improvisation fell apart after 12 bars or so, but it was enough to know that there was something there to keep working on. "Robert even came in singing on it straight away," enthused Jimmy.

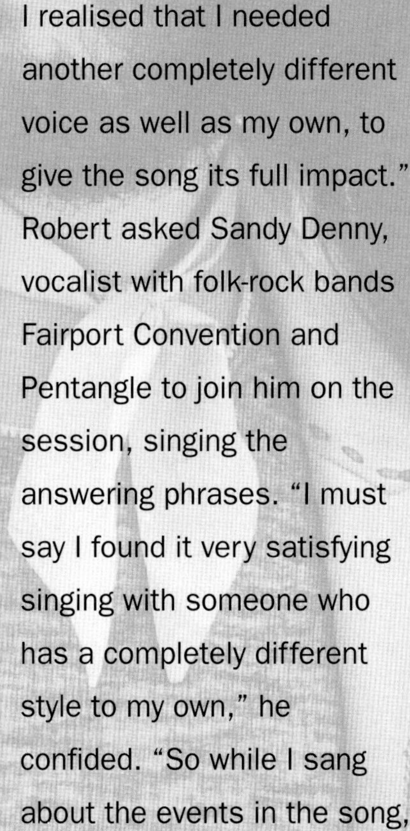

Basically an uptempo 12 bar blues riff, *Rock And Roll* nevertheless features the band playing as a tight and confident outfit. Bonham opens the proceedings with a fierce battery on his Ludwig snare and takes the number out with a 'falling down the stairs' flail round the kit. Page's Telecaster solo hints at Chuck Berry and also at *Heartbreaker* from 'Zep II', while Plant's "...been a long time, been a long time, been a long lonely, lonely, lonely, lonely, lonely time..." will remain one of rock's classic soundbites.

The first two tracks on 'IV' were band compositions but *The Battle Of Evermore* came from Plant and Page. "I'd been reading a book on the Scottish wars just before going to Headley Grange," recalled Plant. "After I'd written the lyrics I realised that I needed another completely different voice as well as my own, to give the song its full impact." Robert asked Sandy Denny, vocalist with folk-rock bands Fairport Convention and Pentangle to join him on the session, singing the answering phrases. "I must say I found it very satisfying singing with someone who has a completely different style to my own," he confided. "So while I sang about the events in the song, Sandy answered back as if she was the pulse of the people on the battlements." Sandy Denny was to later die from injuries sustained during a fall at home.

Page played mandolin on the track; he'd stayed up one night at the Grange and messed around on Jones's instrument. "It was my first experiment with mandolin," he admitted, a little worried at the possible naivety of his playing on something so

unfamiliar. "I suppose all mandolin players would have a great laugh," he fretted, "because it must be the standard thing to play those chords."

If Jimmy was worried about playing overly familiar refrains then track four of 'Led Zeppelin IV' might well have seemed destined to haunt him forever. *Stairway To Heaven* is a veritable goldmine of Page hooks, from the unforgettable acoustic intro (with Jones on recorder) to the electric 12 string middle sections and the chords beneath the solo and playout verse (reminiscent of Hendrix's version of the Dylan song *All Along The Watchtower*).

Stairway was a masterpiece from Page, both compositionally and production-wise. He had used many of the ideas before, but never were they to come together as perfectly as here. "I thought *Stairway...* crystallised the essence of the band," he said later. "It had everything there and showed the band at its best."

Emanating from an original home demo, Jimmy toiled on the track alone one night at the Grange. "Bonzo and Robert had gone out and I worked really hard on the thing," recalled the guitarist. "Jonesy and I then routined it together and later we ran through it with drums and everything." During those rehearsals Plant sat by the open fire, furiously scribbling on a scrap of paper. "He was just sort of writing away," remarked Jimmy, "and suddenly there it was."

TOP LEFT PICTURE

"White Summer"

MAIN PICTURE

"Misty Mountain Hop"

Plant concurred: "Yeah, I just sat next to Pagey while he was playing it through. It took a little working out, but it was a very fluid, unnaturally easy track." It was as though some divine help was at hand: "There was something pushing it," agreed the singer, "saying, 'You guys are okay, but if you want to do something *timeless*, here's a wedding song for you'."

John Paul's bass playing on this track is superb, both tonally and in his choice of notes, and when Bonham enters halfway through – a deliberate dose of dynamics instigated by Page – the tension becomes almost unbearable. Jimmy's solo, for which he brought out the 1958 Telecaster once more, shows a masterful display of what's right for the track; it builds through the chords, with overdubbed slide guitar adding to the mood and Bonham's massive tom and snare fills pushing the song to its climax.

This track would become the band's closing stage number, their most successful single song, a milestone and perhaps also a millstone around their necks. Due to endless radio plays it became so well known and loved by the general public that Plant, in particular, grew to resent it. His lyrics, which had once summed up the views of a generation, now seemed trite and naive and he refused to sing the song in later years, only grudgingly agreeing to perform it at Live Aid in 85 and the Atlantic reunion of 1988.

Jimmy ordered a special Gibson EDS1275 double-neck guitar so he could play the song live. This would become the *Stairway* instrument and one of rock's great icons. Having both six and 12 string necks the EDS1275 allowed Page to play an amalgam of the many guitar parts on the record.

After the album's release later that year, Atlantic desperately wanted to release *Stairway...* as an American single. Peter Grant refused. The relative success of *Black Dog/Misty Mountain Hop* (US No 15) and Rock And Roll/Four Sticks (US No 47) would surely have been overshadowed by such a release. But in fact the public's desire to buy the song resulted in 'Led Zeppelin IV' selling like a single, making it the most successful Zeppelin album of all. Another masterstroke from Grant!

Misty Mountain Hop shows Plant back in West Coast mood. His blatantly hippy lyrics over Page and Jones's pop arrangement make for a different kind of Zeppelin song. The track opens with Jones on Fender Rhodes electric piano and displays a mighty drum sound from Bonham and a pleasing harmony guitar solo from Page. Plant would continue to perform this number on his own shows and at reunions with other Zeppelin members.

The many tricky time signature changes in *Four Sticks* made it one of the band's most difficult numbers to get down onto tape. Named so because Bonham used two sticks in each hand, to add even more weight to his floor tom sound, the Page/Plant song finds Robert in stellar vocal form. Fleetwood Mac's *Tusk* would hark back to the insistent rhythm of this track some eight years later, while Jimmy's jangling rhythm guitar sound would be similarly echoed by The Police's Andy Summers.

TOP LEFT PICTURE

Much of Led Zeppelin III was composed on acoustic guitar at the Welsh cottage Bron–Y–Aur.

BOTTOM RIGHT PICTURE

Page cutting loose on the 6 string neck of his Gibson EDS1275.

Singer songwriters such as James Taylor, Stephen Stills and Joni Mitchell were influences for the softer side of many rock acts of the early 70s. For the romantic and purely acoustic *Going To California*, Page's guitar is in dropped D tuning. It features an alternating bass string figure reminiscent of Stills' *Four And Twenty*, from Crosby, Stills, Nash and Young's album 'Déjà Vu'. But the track is in fact an unashamed nod towards Joni. Originally written about Californian earthquakes, it is ironic that a tremor or two was indeed felt when Page, Grant and Andy Johns were mixing tracks for the album at Sunset Sound. Again, set among stronger and heavier tracks, a number such as this sparkles like a gem.
When The Levee Breaks contains the drum sound to end all drum sounds. It has been copied and sampled to grace the records of other, less imaginative artists. Page tells how the mighty tone was created using a brand new Ludwig kit, which

included Paiste cymbals and a gigantic 26 inch bass drum, in the main hall at Headley Grange using just one microphone. Although *Levee* is basically a mid tempo blues bash over mostly one chord, the track is redeemed by its enormous sound, and by spirited performances from the whole band. But as Zeppelin were so often to do, their fourth album played out to one of its weaker tracks.

Following the debut of *Stairway To Heaven* at Ulster Hall, the UK tour took Led Zeppelin on a return trip around the smaller clubs, culminating in a nostalgic gig where it had all begun, at The Marquee. Then it was off to Europe in May and June, where some ugly scenes at Vigorelli Stadium in Milan shook the group and reminded them of their vulnerability.

The band were performing at a concert organised and sponsored by the government. All went well for a few numbers and then the musicians noticed smoke pouring out from the far end of the pitch. "The promoter then came on stage and told us to tell the kids to stop lighting fires," recounted Page, "and like twits we did. We warned them that the authorities might make us stop playing if there were any more fires." Zeppelin continued playing for another half hour and each time the audience stood for an encore the smoke would billow up from the ground. They repeated their fire warnings until a canister landed about twenty feet from the stage. "We realised then that it wasn't smoke at all," said a horrified Page, "the police were firing bloody tear gas into the crowd. It wasn't until the wind brought it right over to us that we realised what was happening."

A bottle was thrown at the police and that was enough to spark a riot. The band fled the stage but their only escape was through a gas filled tunnel. Page: "We had no idea what would be on the other side but we got through and locked ourselves in our dressing room. All kinds of people were trying to break in, probably thinking it was immune from the rest of it. And we'd left the roadies running around, trying to save our equipment!"

Fortunately the riot gained little worldwide press coverage, but it was events like these – along with tales of fights, motorcycles in hotel corridors and all night orgies – which would begin to haunt the band. From now on their notoriety – either real or exaggerated – would precede them wherever they travelled.

Next came a short American tour, commencing in Vancouver again but this time closing in Honolulu, where the Zeps took a Hawaiian break before their first visit to Japan. This five day tour included a charity concert in Hiroshima. Bonham remarked on the fantastic reception that the band received in Japan: "It was just a fantastic place to play," he said. "The people were so friendly. It turned out that *Immigrant Song* is one of the biggest favourites in Japan and it's the number we always open with. So the audiences were going potty right from the start." The manager of the Tokyo Hilton

MAIN PICTURE

"We thought it was about time people heard something about us, other than that we were eating women and throwing the bones out of the window."

also went potty, banning the group for life due to their after show exuberance!

In October Led Zeppelin flew home, but Plant and Page returned to the Far East for a holiday, taking in Thailand, India and Hong Kong. "In Bankok all the kids followed us," smiled Plant, "calling us 'Billy Boy, Billy Boy' – which means queer – because of our long hair. But they are laughing and happy all the time." Robert and Jimmy loved the feel of the East and its music, elements of which would continually crop up in their song writing.

On November 11th a full UK tour opened at Newcastle City Hall. Continuing for over a month it included two, five-hour marathons at the Empire Pool Wembley (now the Arena), with bands Bronco, Home and Stone The Crows and ended on December 15th at Salisbury.

During the tour the anonymous, unnamed and unheralded fourth album was released. Various music papers had run weekly advertisements showing each band member's runic symbol in turn. This alerted the diehards and the record was a runaway success, entering the UK chart at No 1 and staying in *Billboard*'s American listing longer than any other Zeppelin album. Although failing to dislodge Carole King's 'Tapestry' from the US top spot, the record did confound Atlantic's predictions of commercial doom by becoming the band's all time best seller. And wasn't 'Led Zeppelin V' just around the corner?

PICTURE BELOW

Unleaded and unplugged.

MAIN PICTURE

Old man of rock?

Senior
Citizen
15%OFF
IDENTIFICATION REQUIRED

'Houses Of The Holy' Are You Serious?

By 1972 Led Zeppelin were arguably the biggest act on the world's stages. But their success and notoriety had so far come without recourse to PR agencies or publicists. Again, the secrecy worked both ways, for while it guaranteed the band members the seclusion they craved, those stories which did emerge were generally of the 'boozing, brauling, bonking' type. In fact, such was their reputation that when Peter Grant introduced himself to Bob Dylan at an LA party with, "Hello, I'm Peter Grant, manager of Led Zeppelin," Dylan's telling retort was, "I don't come to you with *my* problems, do I?"

February saw the band off to the East again, this time to Singapore where a single date was scheduled. But the length of the musicians' hair was to prove a deterrent to the Singapore immigration authorities. They turned Zeppelin back, presumably on the grounds that the entrance of such 'Billy Boys' into their country could only serve to corrupt the youth of the nation.

Next came a massively successful Australian tour. In the ten days that the band were there the Antipodeans fell for Zeppelin just as American, British, Japanese and European audiences had done. On the way home Robert and Jimmy stopped off in India to record some experimental pieces with the Bombay Symphony Orchestra.

For the fifth album the band decided to record at Mick Jagger's country estate, Stargroves, again with the aid of The Rolling Stones' mobile. Many new songs had been coming together on the road and during the group's rest periods. Some band members now had home studios and so individual ideas were being committed to tape. And when the four finally assembled at Stargroves there was a fair amount that could be routined quite quickly.

Page: "We just recorded the ideas each one of us had at that particular time. It was simply a matter of getting together and letting it come out."

MAIN PICTURE

Hots on for nowhere.

ABOVE PICTURE

Wearing and Tearing.

Jimmy didn't like the sound at Stargroves, although much of the ground work was completed there. So Zeppelin moved to Olympic, where many of their best tracks had been recorded. When work was complete, the album was mixed partly at Olymbic but finished off at New York's Electric Lady, during the band's eighth US tour.

The record's cover caused problems and delays yet again. By now the title 'Houses Of The Holy' had been chosen in favour of 'Led Zeppelin V'. The name was a romanticised description of the venues the group performed in around the world and the audiences who filled them.

The cover was to be a collage and featured what appeared to be a group of naked children ascending a mystical, rocky landscape. There were in fact only two children, a girl and a boy, Samantha and Stefan Gates, whose photos were superimposed in a variety of positions across the album's gatefold. The problem came with the colours: "The sky started to look like an ad for Max Factor lipstick," complained Jimmy, "and the children looked as though they'd turned purple from the cold." In fact the strange colouring probably adds to the surreal nature of the picture. As with the previous album, the sleeve was to remain devoid of blurb.

The year continued with Zeppelin flying to America once more, where their tour took up most of June. With the recording of the new album complete, the Zeps gave themselves a two month vacation, before it was back to Japan for the second time.

During this year Plant and Page were to receive a royal summons; they were invited to meet The King. The King in question was Elvis Presley, a great hero to both Jimmy and Robert – remember it was Elvis's *Baby Let's Play House* that had fired the young Page into taking up the guitar seriously. The duo were taken to Presley's Las Vegas hotel suite where Elvis, surrounded by his usual entourage of bodyguards and hangers on, proceeded to ignore them. Page became twitchy, not knowing quite what to do in the presence of his idol and feeling like he didn't want to be there at all. Then, after what seemed like an eternity, Presley turned to Jimmy and Robert and said: "Is it true, these stories about you boys on the road?" Plant was quick to gauge the humour in the question, or perhaps to see that he had nothing to lose by offering his own wit in reply: "Of course not," he grinned, "we're family men. I get the most pleasure out of walking hotel corridors singing your songs." Robert then launched into his best version of an Elvis classic: "Ter-reat me like a foooool, ter-reat me mean and cruuuel, bu-hu-hut love me..." The King paused for several interminable seconds and then burst out laughing. The tension was broken as his aides immediately aped their boss's hysterics. Jimmy and Robert remained in his suite for two hours. Elvis had never heard their records, he said, although he did like *Stairway To Heaven*, which his

TOP PICTURE
Moby Dick!

stepbrother had played him. As the two Zeps were walking back down the hotel corridor, discussing their meeting with one of the few rock artists to rank even higher than they did, a voice from behind made them jump. "Hey," called Presley, who had stuck his head out of the door, "Ter-reat me like a foooool..."

'Houses Of The Holy' begins in truly fine style with one of Page's most engaging and hypnotic inventions. *The Song Remains The Same* started life as a home recording which would have been titled *The Overture*, had Plant not decided to add lyrics to the tune. Reminiscent of something The Who's Pete Townshend might devise, with its suspended chords and Telecaster and Rickenbacker 12 string jangle, Jones's bass playing is redolent too of John Entwistle's best melodic work with that group. The differences become apparent as Page's quickfire guitar solo bursts in, before the slowdown in tempo when Plant's unmistakable vocal tone tells you this can only be one band (although Queen would echo the feeling on this and other Zeppelin tracks some years hence).

Page would use the Gibson twin neck for live versions of this song, taking advantage of the guitar's ability to switch both halves on at once: "You leave the 12 string neck open, as far as the sound goes," explained the guitarist; "you play on the six string neck and the 12 string vibrates in sympathy."

Here Jimmy plays some of his most tasteful licks, combining with Bonham's bestial attack on his kick, snare and cymbals to create something which is both gentle and manic. And uniquely Zeppelin. On stage Jimmy would use the Gibson twin neck to emulate the many guitar textures on *The Song Remains The Same.* Plant always loved the track, later saying: "Every time I sing the song, I picture the fact that I've been round and round the world, and at the root of it there's a common denominator for everybody. I'm proud of the lyrics. Somebody pushed my pen for me, I think."

The Rain Song sees John Paul Jones creating superb soundscapes on Mellotron, an early form of synthesiser using looped tapes to reproduce real recorded sounds via a conventional keyboard. The Mellotron was perhaps best known as the instrument used to supply the orchestral sounds on The Moody Blues album 'On The Threshold Of A Dream'.

As well as the sensitive acoustic guitar heard here, Page used his black and white Danelectro electric through an old Supro amplifier; the amp that had been used to record the whole of the first album and which was a common studio companion. Jimmy also employed many unusual tunings, one of his favourites being that used on *Black Mountain Side* from 'Led Zeppelin'. Page: "The low string goes down to B, then A, D, G, A and D. It's like a modal tuning; a sitar tuning in fact." Page was more secretive about how his guitar was tuned for other tracks, saying: "They're my own that I've worked out, so I'd rather keep those to myself."

MAIN PICTURE

Page's solos burst in, ignoring the convention that says blues guitar breaks start slowly and build to a crescendo.

The Rain Song sees Bonham's drumming at its most sensitive, while Jones's bass finds itself in *What Is And What Should Never Be/Ramble On* territory; both busy and inventive. Plant, too, matches the track's gentleness, singing Jimmy's pre-arranged melody, already worked out on his studio at home. It may not be *Whole Lotta Love*, but this track shows the compositional range and true musicality of a band that none of its imitators would come remotely close to.

Although starting out as another acoustic sojourn from Plant and Page, *Over The Hills And Far Away* soon mutates into a powerful rock stomp. The song was released as a US single and reached No 51 on the *Billboard* chart. Jimmy's guitar uses the Leslie organ speaker again and Jones and Bonham display just how tight a rhythm section their constant touring had made them. The fact that home demos were now being made – as opposed to songs being routined and then recorded more or less instantly – is apparent in the polish displayed on this LP.

The Crunge's humour was completely missed by the critics, who obviously felt that a band such as Zeppelin should remain serious in all they did. These narrow minded souls surely underestimated the innate wit in a group whose infamous aftershow banter was based, on their own admission, on 'having a laugh'. They also missed the musical wit, since the James Brown funk (which *The Crunge* parodied so brilliantly) was built around its danceability, whereas the curious time signature in the Zeppelin take-off renders such frivolity impossible.

Eddie Kramer tells a story of how the four Zeps, so delighted with the outcome of *Dancing Days*, promenaded around the lawn at Stargroves during its playback. It certainly contains one of Page's most infectious riffs, once more echoing Eastern themes. The Telecaster's cutting tone is to the fore again, for both conventional and slide playing. Jimmy explained how this guitar, a gift from Jeff Beck and at the time Fender's basic model, was capable of such a diverse range of tones – including that of the much more powerful Les Paul. "It's just different amps, mike placings and all different things," he said. "Also, if you crank it up to distortion point, so you can sustain notes, it's bound to sound like a Les Paul. I was using my Supro amp for the first album and still do. The *Stairway To Heaven* solo was done when I pulled out the Telecaster, which I hadn't used for a long time, plugged it into the Supro and away it went again. That's a different sound entirely from any of the first album."

Whereas The Beatles could get away with their reggae pastiche *Ob-la-di, Ob-la-da*, it was no such luck for the Zeppelins. Again, the detractors couldn't see the *D'yer Mak'er* joke. It came from an old English music hall gag: "My wife's gone to the West Indies." "Jamaica?" "No, she went of her own accord!" Enough said, except that the feel on this track, while totally unauthentic (and let's hope that solo *is* tongue-in-cheek) was so catchy that Plant suggested it be released as a UK single. Mercifully he was talked out of creating a millstone for the band to rival that of Jeff Beck's *Hi Ho Silver Lining*, forever the bane of the guitarist's life.

No Quarter was initially a Jones composition that had been routined as a contender for 'Led Zeppelin IV' the previous year. The new version was slower, and featured John Paul on piano, synthesiser and synth bass. The eerie chords, plus the phasing effect on Plant's voice and the swirling sound of the synthesiser make for a most evocative track. Page's solo is like nothing he'd ever played with Zeppelin before; using a warm, jazzy tone and jazzy licks he weaves his way through the chords with ease. Jimmy liked solitude in the studio when recording his guitar. Other band members were not allowed to watch. "Never," he stated. "I don't like anybody else in the studio when I'm putting on the guitar parts. I usually just limber up for a while and maybe do just three solos and take the best of the three." And mistakes? "I'll always leave the mistakes in. I can't help it."

'Houses Of The Holy' finishes with *The Ocean*, an ode to the sea of fans to which Plant and

MAIN PICTURE

Achilles Last Stand!

company had performed so many times. Written using alternate bars of 4/4 and 7/8, the song might be expected to sound cumbersome or twitchy. But such was the skill in its composition, execution and production that it manages not to alienate the listener. Only when the guitar solo swings in using a standard 'walking' feel does any contrast manifest itself.

Though perhaps not one of the fans' favourite albums (of the eight Zeppelin UK No 1s it spent the least time in the charts), 'Houses Of The Holy' is in fact an excellent record. Documenting the band's maturity as players and composers, and yet neither slick nor over produced, it stands as a fine testament to four musicians who still loved each other and the music they made. Plant's caustic side swipe at the critics said it all: "So there's some buggers that don't like the album," he joshed. "Well, God bless 'em. I like it and there's a few thousand other buggers like it too."

'Houses Of The Holy' was completed and mixed during November 72, as news broke of a two month UK tour. This was Zeppelin's longest ever outing in their own country and 100,000 tickets were sold in a single day. The tour began once more at Newcastle City hall, on the last day of November. It would not finish until early 1993, a year of huge highs for the band but the start of some lows that would sap their combined strength and lead, inevitably, to their downfall.

'Physical Graffiti' Double Dealing

As the band's hardest ever UK tour drew to a close in January 73, with Robert developing flu and Zeppelin having to reschedule the final dates in Bradford and Preston, the planned February release of 'Houses Of The Holy' was put back due to design problems. The group took the month off before setting out on a four week tour across Europe, beginning in Copenhagen on March 3rd. During the tour, and almost a year after recording had first started, the album was finally released.

On May 4th the group set off for their ninth US visit. This was to be the big one. The band had rehearsed a brand new stage and lighting rig to take with them on this massive two legged jaunt, and for the first time they hired their own jet. Travelling around America, with often vast distances between cities, would be far easier from now on – and a good deal more prestigious, since their plane was larger than Air Force One, President Richard Nixon's own private jet. The Boeing 720B, or The Starship, as it became known, was a further symbol of Led Zeppelin's status as the world's number one band. Painted in blue and dotted with white stars, The Starship also had 'Led Zeppelin' arrogantly emblazoned along its fuselage. But the Zeps were not the only ones who could afford their own wings. Page recalled a certain group of ladies in Texas: "Down there they've got the richest groupies in the world," he quipped. "Some of them followed our jet in their private jet!"

The tour kicked off in Atlanta, at The Braves Stadium, where Zeppelin played to just under 50,000 fans. It was the following night that The Beatles' longstanding Shea Stadium record was broken. During this first leg Page sprained his finger, making playing difficult and resulting in the group's LA Forum date being shifted. A short holiday in Hawaii and leg two of the tour began.

As the second half kicked off in Chicago, filming began on what was to become a feature length film of the band's exploits. Eventually to be named 'The Song Remains The Same', the project was the idea of film maker Joe Massot. Massot had approached the band and their manager earlier in the tour and suggested he film the shows. Initially turned down by Grant, Massot was subsequently contacted by the team and he began shooting backstage and testing out ideas during performances at Baltimore and Pittsburgh.

The tour culminated in three prestigious dates at Madison Square Garden on July 27th, 28th and

MAIN PICTURE

Zeppelin: a band of "unquestionable individual talent".

29th. These shows were filmed in their entirety and provided a mass of footage that was edited down to become the finished product. Engineer Eddie Kramer recorded the gigs – the sound was remixed in New York and London – and the tapes became the basis for the film soundtrack and album of the same name.

While the performances were full of the usual Zeppelin gusto, they hardly represented the pinnacle of the group's musical perfection. As ever, Page was pragmatic: "You've got to be reasonably honest with it," he shrugged. "It wasn't the best concert, playing-wise, but it was the only one with celluloid footage. So there it was. For all the mistakes and everything else, it's a very honest filmtrack. It was just, 'There you are, take it or leave it'."

On the middle of the three Madison Square Garden gigs, an event occurred which gained much public attention at the time and caused great upheaval in the camp. $203,000 had been left by tour manager Richard Cole and attorney Steve Weiss in a safety deposit box at the Drake Hotel, to pay for tour expenses such as The Starship, crew wages etc. As the band left for the show the money was discovered missing, although Plant, Page and Jones only found out when they came off stage during Bonzo's solo in *Moby Dick.*

Plant and Page took the theft in their stride – they could afford it, they reasoned. "Jimmy and I just laughed about it," admitted Robert. "Bonzo did go a bit berserk, but for Jimmy and me it all somehow made sense. There was nothing else you could do but laugh, really."

Richard Cole took a lie detector test which eliminated him as a suspect (it was implied by some that he'd staged the robbery himself) and Peter Grant was arrested for striking a photographer during a press conference. But Plant's main concern was with the intrusion by outsiders into their lives. "The big drag was the flipout with the media," he said, "pouring into our bedrooms, taking pictures and asking questions. That reminded me of being knifed or something, and lying in your room getting your last breath while some guy is trying to get it on film or into a newspaper. That part of it was ghastly."

Although a $10,000 reward was offered for information leading to the recovery of the cash, the crime remained unsolved. Ironically, for this tour Zeppelin had finally resorted to hiring a PR agency, in order to gain the higher profile they felt some groups of lesser stature were gaining – particularly The Stones. Plant: "We knew full well we were doing more business than them. We were getting better gates in comparison to a lot of people who were constantly glorified in the press. So, without getting egocentric, we thought it was about time people heard something about us,

MAIN PICTURE

Page backstage: "I start biting my nails and telling people to leave me alone."

69

other than that we were eating women and throwing the bones out of the window."

In October Joe Massot (who was eventually replaced by Australian Peter Clifton, due to the band not liking the early rushes) visited Britain and filmed the various members of the band going about their private lives, including Bonham Drag racing at Santa Pod and Jimmy climbing hills near his home at Loch Ness in Scotland. The house, once owned by occultist Aleister Crowley (known as The Great Beast) was built on the same plot as a church in which the congregation had burned to death while the building was razed to the ground by fire.

Page's interests in things mystical would be blamed by some for the many tragedies to befall the band in coming years. Jimmy never hid his fascination with the occult but always claimed it was just that, although at about this time he did open a bookshop in Kensington dealing with such matter. "My studies have been quite intensive," he admitted, "but I don't particularly want to go into it because it's a personal thing and doesn't relate to anything, apart from the fact that I've employed his system in my own day to day life." Crowley's system was based around the liberation of the person from the constraints of daily life, saying that such restriction of the soul can lead to frustration, violence, mental sickness, crime and so forth. "I'm not trying to interest anyone else in Aleister Crowley," insisted Page, "any more than I am in Charles Dickens. All it was, was that at a particular time he was expounding a theory of self liberation. He was like an eye to the world, into the forthcoming situation. But it's those things people attacked him on, so he was misunderstood."

As 1973 faded out, the group were once again at Headley Grange, where Page and Bonham rehearsed and recorded a track which would later become the epic *Kashmir*. Recording broke off suddenly when (as it was told at the time) Jones became ill and needed a rest. In fact, John Paul had told Peter Grant that he had had enough of the whole thing and was quitting the band. Grant told him to take a break over Christmas and come back having mulled things over. When Jones returned he had decided to stay. Future Zeppelin projects would see a far greater involvement from the bassist, especially in the musical arrangements, since he felt the band needed to diversify if they were to survive.

May 1974 saw a new development. At this time their five year contract with Atlantic came up for renewal and in negotiating the new deal Grant insisted that all future Zeppelin records be released on their own label. With offices in Chelsea and Manhatten the new label would be called Swan Song; it would not only look after the interests of its main act but would also sign other artists. These included Bad Company, The Pretty Things, Maggie Bell and later Dave Edmunds. The label's first No 1 record came with Bad Company's eponymously titled debut release.

As usual, various names had been suggested for the new label, including Slut, Slag and Stairway,

but the title eventually came from Page. "I had a long acoustic guitar instrumental with just a sparse vocal section," he elaborated. "We were recording with the truck (the mobile studio) and there was no title for it and someone shouted out, 'What's it going to be called?' I shouted back *Swan Song* and the whole thing stopped. We said what a great name for the LP. Then all the vibes started and suddenly it was out of the LP and on to the record label." Page felt the name was a good one – should a Swan Song artist fail, then the title became more than a little appropriate!

Robert detailed his vision of the kind of company Swan Song would be: "The label won't just be Led Zeppelin," he asserted. "It's too much effort to do as an ego trip, and a waste of time really. We're going to work with people we've known and we've liked, and people we will know and will like. It's an outlet for people we admire and want to help. We want to take some artists who we think are fine, and never let them down at any point. That's our intention."

The label was launched with two lavish parties, one at the Four Seasons restaurant in New York (costing $10,000) and the other at the Bel Air Hotel in LA, where stars of the rock and film worlds rubbed shoulders.

The first Led Zeppelin release on Swan Song would be 'Physical Graffiti', the band's first double album. Page: "As usual, we had more material than the required 40 odd minutes for one album" – in fact they had an album and a half's

MAIN PICTURE

Plant: "Tours are exhausting, no doubt about that."

worth – "so we figured let's put out a double and use some of the material we had done previously but never released. *Black Country Woman* and *Rover* were done at the same time as we did *D'Yer Mak'er*, *Bron-Y-Aur* was done for 'Zeppelin III'; *Down By The Seaside, Night Flight* and *Boogie With Stu* were from the sessions for the fourth album."

Many regard this as the quintessential Led Zeppelin collection. It contains every facet of the band's considerable talent. Each shade and colour in their rich musical palette is here; from riffy rockers to folksy ballads and from Eastern blockbusters to funky jams.

Record one blasts open with *Custard Pie*. Recorded for the album at Headley Grange (this time they used Ronnie Lane's mobile studio), *Custard Pie* is dominated by Bonham's monster drum sound and a seriously good rhythm guitar riff from Page. It's not, however, one of Zeppelin's most harmonically inventive numbers. The track also demonstrates how Plant's vocals were for some reason mixed too low on all the fresh Headley Grange material.

The Rover started life as an acoustic blues piece, but the band turned it into this raunchy rocker at Stargroves, originally for inclusion on 'Houses Of The Holy'. Jones's bass pumps out the rhythm while Jimmy's guitar riff in E is his most overdriven and intentionally distorted yet. The unusually measured solo (unusual for Page, at any rate) is reminiscent of Clapton's guitar break in Cream's *Badge*. A curious 'credit' on the record sleeve reads 'Guitar lost courtesy Nevison. Salvaged by the grace of Harwood'. This refers to Ron Nevison and Keith Harwood, two of the engineers who worked on the album. Did Nevison erase a track of guitar and Harwood somehow restore it? The chief engineer on Mike Oldfield's 'Tubular Bells' was actually credited on more than one album as Tom 'Bulk Erase' Newman', for accidentally putting all sixteen tracks into record and wiping the lot. So Roy shouldn't feel *too* bad.

Some of the slide guitar on *In My Time Of Dying* takes us back to 'Led Zeppelin II', although this track was recorded at Headley Grange in 1974. An adaptation of a traditional folk blues, *In My Time Of Dying* features the definitive Bonham sound; the loudest bass drum on record and a snare that rings out like gunshots in the dark. The basic rhythm track of guitar, bass and drums was always laid down as a three piece unit. Bonham's cry of "That's got to be the one hasn't it?" shows that this take felt right. In fact it's hard to see how it could have been bettered – shortened, perhaps, but not bettered.

Strangely, the title track to 'Houses Of The Holy' didn't appear on that album. Instead it was held over and takes its place here alongside *Black Country Woman* from the same Stargroves sessions. The guitar intro fools the listener into thinking this is going to be Zeppelin at their exciting best, but although Plant's vocals are strong and the band as tight as ever, the overall result is somewhat mundane.

Stevie Wonder's *Superstition* was actually written for Jeff Beck, although the composer eventually chose to use it first. *Trampled Underfoot* employs a similar funk riff and is likewise played on a Hohner Clavinet, a sort of electric harpsichord. The vocals again are too low in the mix, and for all its great feel the track would have benefited from a minute or so shaved from its 5.35 length. *Trampled Underfoot* was considered strong enough to be released as a single in America, where it reached No 38 on the *Billboard* chart. A special pressing was also made to coincide with the band's shows in Earls Court in May 75.

Track six exemplified the brilliance of Led Zeppelin. Without recourse to blazing guitar solos and power chords *Kashmir* manages to be one of the heaviest songs in rock. "It's all there," agreed Jones, "all the elements that defined the band." Page admitted later that professional string and horn players were brought in to supplement the group, an almost unheard of state of affairs with Zeppelin.

Page and Bonham had already routined the number, originally born out of Jimmy's *Black Mountain Side* tuning and sounding for all the world like a Sultan's funeral dirge. Both Page and Plant have described the thoughts that went into creating the song. Jimmy: "I had this idea to combine orchestra and Mellotron and have them duplicate the guitar parts. Jonesy improvised whole sections with the Mellotron and added the final, ascending riff, whereby the song fades." Plant devised the lyrics on a long journey from Goulimine to Tantan, in southern Morocco. "The whole inspiration came from the fact that the road went on and on," he related. "It was a single track road cut through the desert; two miles east and west were ridges of sandrock. It basically looked like you were driving down a channel, this dilapidated road, and there was seemingly no end to it." The song contains one of Robert's favourite lyrics: "'Oh, let the sun beat down upon my face, stars to fill my dreams'." *All My Love* and *In The Light* also rate as Plant highlights in the Zeppelin catalogue. "But *Kashmir* was the one," he insisted. "It was so positive." Kashmir received its debut in Rotterdam on January 11 1975 and was played at every show until the band's final performance on July 7th 1980.

The second disc begins with *In The Light*, another Eastern sounding, mystical piece. It opens with Jones on ethereal keyboards and sees Plant singing about positivity and optimism. As well as being one of Robert's best loved numbers, Page has also stated that it was his favourite from this entire selection.

Originally slated for 'Led Zeppelin III', *Bron-Y-Aur* is a pretty, if rather throwaway acoustic guitar exercise from Jimmy.

The Neil Young influence is clearly audible in the next track, *Down By The Seaside*, with its country style guitar and loping feel. John Paul Jones plays some sensitive electric piano, while the tempo change is actually reminiscent of Paul McCartney's James Bond movie theme *Live And Let Die.* The McCartney soundalike continues with *Ten Years Gone*, whose chords, tempo changes and harmony guitars are redolent of the ex Beatle's epic *Band*

On The Run. This was Plant's missive about an ex-girlfriend who gave him the classic musician's ultimatum – 'It's me or the band'. Robert: "I said 'I can't stop, I've got to keep going'." Plant went on to describe how content the girl might be these days, perhaps with an automatic washing machine and a little sports car. "I could probably relate to her," he suggested, "but she couldn't relate to me. Ten years gone, I'm afraid."

Swan Song signing, Dave Edmunds, would have been proud of the next one. Originally intended as a fourth album inclusion, *Night Flight* conjures up the feel of Edmunds' No 1 hit, *I Hear You Knockin'*. Jones is back on Hammond organ here.

The Wanton Song is one of the cleverest tracks on the record, in every respect. This powerhouse of riffs and machine gun tempo changes is tempered by subtle chords and a wealth of arrangement and production ideas. Plant sings evocatively of young girls and Page adds superb Leslie guitar and some spine tingling backwards power chords. The rhythm section could surely not be bettered on this.

In contrast, *Boogie With Stu* is three and a half minutes of bland fun, recorded initially for 'Led Zeppelin IV'. 'Stu' is the late Ian Stewart, often known as the fifth Stone. Stewart was The Rolling Stones' road manager and often played keyboards with the band.

Jimmy enjoyed the double album format as it allowed the band the luxury of including tracks such as this and *Bron-Y-Aur*, which might otherwise have been (indeed were!) left out of a single record's track listing.

The intro dialogue to the wholly acoustic *Black Country Woman* shows how this take was nearly aborted due a light plane flying over Stargroves (the track was a spring 72 recording). Page had decided the garden might be an interesting place to try out a song and had set microphones up to capture the number live. The Plant lament about one more love gone wrong originally ended with him saying, "What's the matter with you mama; never ending, doubting woman blues," but the final line was cut from the track. This was also the US B-side to *Trampled Underfoot*.

Sick Again details the groupie mayhem of previous tours. Sounding for all the world like an out-take from 'Led Zeppelin II' the song was actually a brand new recording, made at Headley Grange in 1974. It featured purposeful performances from the whole band. Bonzo, Page and Jones work brilliantly together in the rhythm section, while Jimmy's overdubbed slide guitar fills and solo (including mistakes) could not have been more appropriate. A great vocal performance here from Robert sees the album out in stomping style. Just for a change the new record's release would be delayed due to artwork problems with the sleeve. This depicted a New York tenement building (96 St Marks) with the windows replaced by photos, paintings and various icons chosen by the band as significant or humorous. Page came up with the 'Physical Graffiti' title: "Because of the whole thing of graffiti on the album cover and it being a physical statement rather than a written one. I feel that an awful lot of physical energy is used in producing an album," he stated.

MAIN PICTURE
"The best bloody band there was."

The rest of 1974 was an unusually quiet time for the band. Although there were no tours and recording for the forthcoming album was complete, various members found time to jam with other acts: Jones put together the band for Roy Harper's free Hyde Park gig, with Dave Gilmour and Steve Broughton; Jimmy and John Paul both jammed with Bad Company at shows in England and America; and Page and Bonham sat in with Crosby, Stills and Nash at an afternoon session in London.

Before Christmas the group got together to rehearse a set for their tenth tour of America, due to begin at the Metro Sports Centre in Minneapolis on January 18th 1975. The year was to prove both triumphant and traumatic for the band, who were riding a runaway train of success. But was the train gathering too much momentum? Was it out of control?

Presence’ Back To The Basics

Before they set off to America yet again, the band performed two warm-up dates in Europe. The first of these was in Rotterdam on January 11th. The following night saw Zeppelin in Brussels, where DJ Bob Harris interviewed Robert for BBC2’s Old Grey Whistle Test.

Just days before Page was due to start the six week spring tour – during which time he would play to more than a million people – he trapped his finger in a train door at London’s Victoria station. This forced Zeppelin to convene in Minneapolis to rehearse a revised set; Jimmy removed *Dazed And Confused*, as the guitar playing, string bending in particular, proved difficult and painful. The song returned to the show a fortnight later at Madison Square Garden.

For the first few dates Robert also had flu (for which a gig in St Louis was cancelled), but once this and Jimmy’s injury were overcome the first leg of the tour went relatively smoothly. The Zeppelin rig was now massive, with 40 crew and security men, 150 lights (including three krypton lasers and a neon ‘Led Zeppelin’ sign), dry ice machines and a 70,000 watt, computerised sound system. Once more the group availed themselves of The Starship.

Such was the demand for tickets that rioting became a problem outside certain venues. Fighting erupted between fans and the police in Boston and the show was cancelled; and at Greensboro in North Carolina the band had to make a dash for their lives after the show, with Peter Grant at the wheel of one of the limos!

During the break between legs one and two of the tour, ‘Physical Graffiti’ was released to fantastic acclaim. The two year wait had been worth it. In the UK the album went straight to the top, while in America it entered at three, before climbing to No 1 where it remained for six weeks. Amazingly, the previous five albums also re-entered the *Billboard* chart, making Led Zeppelin the most successful rock act ever in the United States.

Due to the ‘Graffiti’ madness now sweeping the States, the second half of the tour went extraordinarily well. Bad Company (and ex-Free) drummer Simon Kirke jammed with the band on the March 7th gig at Austin, Texas. The following day should have seen Zeppelin playing to 150,000 fans at Florida’s West Palm Beach Speedway, but the show was cancelled due to logistical problems. Deep Throat porn star Linda Lovelace was hired to introduce Led Zeppelin on stage for the final dates at the LA Forum. The Los Angeles crowds were ecstatic. It had been the group’s most jubilant and artistically rewarding visit yet. Plant said of the trip: “Looking back on it, this tour’s been a flash.

MAIN PICTURE

Zeppelin undertook a one-band Blitzkrieg of the world.

Really fast. Very poetic too. Lots of battles and conquests, backdropped by the din of the hordes. Aside from the fact that it's been our most successful tour on every level, I found myself having a great time all the way through. The music's gelled amazingly well. Everyone loved 'Physical Graffiti' and that meant a lot." Robert knew nothing of the trauma that was soon to grip the band as he continued: "It's like we're on an incredible winning streak."

Meanwhile, tickets for a three day stint at London's Earls Court had gone on sale in the UK and sold out within four hours. Two extra dates were soon added and the gigs, to be held between the 17th and 25th of May, would be seen by 85,000 British fans. Earls Court's size meant that at last British concert goers could witness the full Zeppelin spectacle which American audiences had been thrilling to for years. The dates were an outrageous success, seen as a watershed by both the group and their usual pack of carping critics.

Next day the band dispersed. They were now tax exiles from their own country and so left to take what they believed would be a couple of relaxing months holiday, before the scheduled return to America in August. Plant and his wife Maureen went travelling to Morocco, where they were met by Jimmy in Marrakesh for the Moroccan folk festival. Plant and Page hired a Range Rover and drove through the country, revelling in the local music and gleaning inspiration for music yet to be written.

MAIN PICTURE

Jimmy Page with ubiquitous cigarette.

The band eventually met up in Montreux before Robert joined his family on the Greek island of Rhodes. Jimmy took a brief trip to London to check the progress of the film, which Peter Clifton was still working on. Privately the band were strongly thinking about scrapping this less than perfect project, shooting new footage and recording new shows on the August tour. Events, however, removed such an option.
On August 4th Plant's car left a winding mountain road and hit a tree. Robert suffered a severely broken ankle and damage to both elbows. He would be in a wheelchair for some time. Maureen came off even worse, with a badly fractured skull and pelvis. At first Plant thought his wife was dead: "I looked across at Maureen and thought she had stopped breathing," he said. "She was in a terrible state." The couple and their two children, Karac and Carmen, who had been in the back of the car and so escaped serious injury, were taken to hospital by open fruit truck. "It was so low that my leg trailed along the ground," remarked Robert. With Maureen so badly hurt, the family needed more than the basic medical assistance available on the island, so they were flown back to England where they were tended to in comfort. But while in the little Greek hospital it was brought home to Plant just how widespread the Zeppelin legend had become. Robert: "I was lying there in some pain, trying to get cockroaches off the bed, when the guy next to me, this drunken soldier, started singing *The Ocean* from 'Houses Of The Holy'!

Due to the prevailing tax problem Robert couldn't stay in London and so took off to Jersey in the Channel Islands, where he was safe from the taxman but less than an hour's flight for the London specialists who visited him regularly. Robert was told that he wouldn't walk again for six months and so, as soon as his leg got better, he moved to Malibu beach to recuperate in the

California sun. Page joined him and the two set about writing a new collection of songs. Not unnaturally, 'Presence' was to reflect the darker moments brought about by Plant's accident and its aftermath.

When Jones and Bonham joined the pair in Malibu in October, Robert and Jimmy had already sketched out most of the tracks. Almost the entire album would consist of Page/Plant compositions. Rehearsals at Hollywood's SIR Studios soon knocked the set into shape and the band flew to Munich, where recording would take place at one of Jimmy's favourite venues, Musicland.

Everything happened very quickly. "The whole band really wanted to play and had wanted to do that tour," said Robert, "so the same effort was put into the album." Plant was still in plaster, and not only was the action of singing painful, but Robert felt stupid sitting in a wheelchair or standing on crutches. He also felt unable to give his usual 101%. "I think my vocal performance on it is pretty poor," admitted the singer. "The saving grace on the album was *Candy Store Rock* and *Achilles Last Stand*. The rhythm section on that was so inspired."

Achilles Last Stand opens the album. Written about Robert and Jimmy's travels just after their amazingly successful Earls Court gigs, the track is an incredible performance by the whole band. Robert's criticism of his singing on the album is perhaps founded on the fact that physical discomfort kept him from reaching his most outrageous notes. But in some ways it benefited the songs, making the lyrics more discernible and the tracks more immediately accessible. Like almost all Zeppelin numbers *Achilles Last Stand* was recorded as a basic live take, with guitar and vocal overdubs added afterwards. This was at a time when groups were beginning to create songs in the studio by layering drums, bass, keyboards and guitars one at a time. If confirmation were needed as to which method breathes most life into a recording, this track is it.

For Your Life sees Jimmy taking up a new guitar. The chordal dive bomb effect heard during the intro and elsewhere in the song shows Page using the tremolo arm on his latest acquisition, a Lake Placid Blue Fender Stratocaster. Page is rare among top guitarists for his uncommon use of the Strat, preferring his Tele, Les Paul or Danelectro. But this single mindedness helped separate him from the crowd. His solo here has real venom, perhaps in response to Robert's feelings of pain and inadequacy; the rhythm section also excels, with Jones and Bonham as funky as ever, underpinning and holding the track together admirably.

Plant's lyrics show just how low he had been feeling. "They were all reflections on the time near and before the accident," he declared, "and that time afterwards, the contemplative thing. I was very determined, lyrically and vocally, and Jimmy put his energy into it. He worked so hard, and the guitar playing on this album surpasses anything I've heard for ages and ages. Brilliant. So much life in it."

Lyrically, *Royal Orleans* describes the antics of a certain gent while staying at this famous hotel in New Orleans. Musically it's another funky workout, full of Page's rhythm guitar and convoluted riffs. It sees Jones's bass powering the track along, with superb skinsmanship from Bonham – especially that hi-hat work.

Guitar and voice mimic each other on *Nobody's Fault But Mine* in true blues style. Blind Willie Johnson was originally responsible for the lyrics, although the song is credited on the album to

Jimmy and Robert. Plant's blues harp solo here is his best, perhaps recorded through a small guitar amp for that authentic gutsy tone. For *Candy Store Rock*, Robert's slapback echo vocal and Jimmy's rock'n'roll guitar licks sit strangely over a Jones/Bonzo funk assault. Something of a filler this, although the band's great feel is undiminished.

"*In Hots On For Nowhere* I was furious with Page and Peter Grant," confessed Robert. "I was just furious that I couldn't get back to the woman and the children that I loved. And I was thinking, 'Is all this rock'n'roll really worth anything at all?'"

In previous albums Zeppelin had been guilty of using the slow blues as a filler. Not so here. The track which ends 'Presence' sees Robert missing his home and family, and especially his wife Maureen, who was still recovering from her near fatal injuries. Hence the moving *Tea For One*. Once more the live band feel provides power and interplay between the musicians. Page's solo here is more heartfelt than on almost any previous Zeppelin blues – *Since I've Been Loving You* being the obvious exception.

'Presence' was recorded in 18 days, by far the shortest time since 'Led Zeppelin'. It was full of energy and dynamics, if a little short on the band's usual diversity. There were no epic production numbers and no acoustic folk songs or Eastern dirges. Here was the greatest live band on earth, wounded, and committing to tape their combined pain and frustration. As Page put it: "'Presence' was pure anxiety and emotion. I mean, we didn't know if we'd ever be able to play in the same way again. It might have been a very dramatic change if the worst had happened to Robert."

The worst nearly did happen. "I was hobbling around in the middle of this great track," he recalled, "when suddenly my enthusiasm got the better of me. I was running to the vocal booth with this orthopaedic crutch when down I went on the bad foot. There was an almighty crack and a great flash of light and pain and I folded up in agony." Plant had never seen Jimmy move so quickly: "He was out of the mixing booth and holding me up, fragile as he might be, within a second. He became quite Germanic in his organisation of things and instantly I was rushed off to hospital again, in case I'd reopened the fracture. If I had, I would have never walked properly again."

When recording had finished, the band retired once more to Jersey, still unable to enter the UK without incurring massive tax liabilities. It was here one night that they delighted 350 punters (and the resident pianist Norman Hale) at Beehan's West Park night club with an impromptu display of rock'n'roll standards and better known Zeppelin classics.

'Presence' was released on April 5th 1976, after yet another round of sleeve problems. In the UK the album went gold immediately, with advance orders among the highest ever, while in America it entered the *Billboard* chart at No 24 and was at the top within a fortnight. The record's sales were somewhat impaired by the release of the film and soundtrack to *The Song Remains The Same* only six months later. But 'Presence' deserves a higher ranking in the Zeppelin album hierarchy than it usually receives. Recorded with the very life of the band in jeopardy, the LP is a huge testimony to the brilliance of Page as a guitarist, producer and mediator. As with The Yardbirds almost a decade earlier, it was Jimmy who held it all together. Without him, 1975 might have seen the demise of Led Zeppelin.

'The Song Remains The Same' Live But Not Kicking

The start of 1976 would find Robert Plant in a state of mending. It would finish with him a broken man.

By spring Robert could walk again. He had taken his first faltering steps on New Year's Day, but his return to the stage came when he and Jimmy joined Bad Company at the LA Forum on May 23rd. It was a relief to all concerned that Robert could move once more, and his performance that night was rapturously received. But from the date of the accident it would take a year for Robert to make a complete recovery.

So it was fortuitous that the film and soundtrack to 'The Song Remains The Same' were in the can and ready to stop the gap created by the band's lack of activity. During the previous months, between tours and the making of 'Presence', Page had assisted Peter Clifton in editing various sequences for the film; he had also sat with Eddie Kramer, working on the soundtrack to ensure that the live set would sound as professional as possible.

Of course it was a compromise. The recordings had been made at the end of a gruelling American tour and in many cases the performances were – like the band on occasion – somewhat frayed at the edges. Page was a little concerned at the scrappy nature of some of the takes, and in particular his guitar solos. As a wholly inspirational musician, Page would have moments of brilliance and others where it just didn't happen, or where something he reached for was missed by a mile. There was a fair bit of this in the soundtrack. "There are loads of howling guitar mistakes on it," admitted Jimmy. "Normally one would be inclined to cut them out, but you can't when it's a soundtrack."

Despite such comments, Page would still be accused of studio sorcery. He would also be targeted by some particularly stupid people as the source of the band's coming troubles.

1976 saw the start of punk in Great Britain and soon it was in full swing. Bands like The Sex Pistols, The Clash and The Damned had arrived, their avowed intent to rid the world of such stadium rock 'dinosaurs' as Yes, Genesis, Queen and of course Led Zeppelin. As a member of The Clash was reported to have said, "I don't even have to listen to their music; just looking at one of their album covers makes me want to vomit."

Zeppelin had no reason to fear the punks. At a time when the British music press clambered aboard the spiky haired bandwagon by the truckload, their own magazines' polls were

MAIN PICTURE

Tall Cool One.

consistently won by Led Zeppelin, and punk record sales would be dwarfed by those of this band alone. Various Zep members later attended the occasional punk gig, just to see what the fuss was all about; Jimmy and Robert caught The Damned's show at Covent Garden's Roxy, and Robert would take Bonzo along to see Eater, Generation X and The Damned at the same venue.

Jimmy enjoyed The Damned. "I was absolutely amazed at the power that was coming out of them," he later declared. Robert said of punk: "As a basic movement it's good, but I wish the music was more original. The Stranglers, for example, sound like an English Doors, pre 'LA Woman'. So that doesn't do much for me or anybody else, really."

Although 'The Song Remains The Same' was released on October 22nd, the work had already been done and so the band found itself in a state of limbo. In fact, there would be a two year gap between their last studio album 'Presence' and their next; a gap which would see Zeppelin's feathers truly ruffled by rumours, half-truths, untruths, tragedy and speculation as to their very existence as a band.

As usual, Jones and Bonham retrenched to their country lairs, hiding away from the spotlight whenever possible. Bonzo did jump on stage with Deep Purple and announce, "Hi, I'm John Bonham from Led Zeppelin and we've got a new album coming out soon!" He also visited Montreux with Page (among rumours that he was leaving Zeppelin and recording a solo album), where the two experimented with a 'percussion only' track. This would later turn up on 'Coda'.

Jones appeared at a Marquee jam with The Pretty Things; unfortunately, Chinese whispers told that Zeppelin were playing a secret gig – perhaps with the thought of establishing some unity. And while it was great for the fans to see Jonesy in action at such close quarters, the lack of Plant, Page and Bonzo will have come as a great disappointment.

Plant and Page both conducted interviews to allay the fears of those who believed the band was on its last legs. Plant commented: "In this band we're very lucky that everybody is more enthusiastic as time goes on. There's no fatigue or boredom musically." Page was more specific: "There's no reason to split up. There's nothing inherent musically in Led Zeppelin to harm or destroy it. There is variety, great freedom and no restrictions on the players whatsoever. Everyone plays something to knock the others out. I can't see any split coming."

'The Song Remains The Same' was premiered in New York, at Cinema One in Manhatten with all four members present. Two days later, to coincide with the release of the soundtrack album, the film was shown for the first time on the West Coast. Parties followed both screenings. Jimmy described the feeling of watching the premiere – a new experience, being in the audience at a Zeppelin concert: "The first time in New York was great," he enthused. "Every time I had seen the film before was with technicians, people with a really critical eye. But then the film really lived for the first time and you could see people getting off on things, applauding and laughing at the right times; generally vibing."

Although 'The Song Remains The Same' received awards from film magazines for Best

Documentary and Best Soundtrack Of The Year, it was slammed by the music press. The band were criticised for touching up the sound and putting right mistakes; they received a further battering as 'egocentrics' and for the unprofessional way the film was put together. Nevertheless, it was a runaway success, packing out cinemas everywhere and providing fans with the opportunity to see the band in private, as well as gaining a front row glimpse of their heroes on one of the world's great stages.

By 1976 the extended guitar solo formula – especially in live album guise – was definitely passé; Cream had been dead seven years now and, what's more, if Zeppelin wanted to play into the hands of their punk loving detractors this was the perfect vehicle. Still, while the trendies hated it even more than 'Presence', 'The Song Remains The Same' still went platinum – before it was even released!

It has been said that listening to this double album is 'a taxing experience' and that's as accurate a description as any. Of course there are highlights. *Rock And Roll* is a worthy opener and *Celebration Day* follows it well. The title track is one of the best takes on the record (in the film you see Plant going through his fantasy sequence) and *The Rain Song,* which segues into it, is a pleasant listen. But *Dazed And Confused* – an expected highlight with Jimmy's violin bow extravaganza and his lick swapping sequence with Plant – is, at almost half an hour, too much even for the most committed fan to take.

No Quarter is a real delight, except that again it's too long. The music gels well and features a fine Page solo. Unfortunately the delicate intro to *Stairway To Heaven* (which actually followed *Dazed...* on the night) is all but drowned out by the audience frenzy induced by that number. This gives an indication of how different the gig must have seemed from a spectator's standpoint and shows why so many of the numbers work better in the film than they do from a purely aural point of view.

If you like drum solos you'll like *Moby Dick*; if you like *long* drum solos you'll love it. The film does at least use this section to show us the private side of Bonzo, but on the record tedium sets in too soon.

Only one song could round off a live album from Led Zeppelin and *Whole Lotta Love* is certainly a highlight. But the film footage of the concert shows how it dovetailed out of *Heartbreaker* (curiously left off the record), and seems to make more of *The Crunge* and *Let That Boy Woogie* sequences.

As a commercial success 'The Song Remains The Same' soundtrack was a smash, with its platinum sales and No 1 status around the world. But as a representation of the greatest live band on earth it is a poor, or perhaps more accurately 'unfortunate' testimony.

In early November, a few days after a massive launch party for the official UK premiere, the first public showings of the film were staged. Simultaneous sellout openings in Birmingham, Cambridge, Glasgow, Leeds, Liverpool, Reading and Southampton confirmed its commercial viability. In 1984 a video version would be released, the perfect complement to a six pack and a takeaway vindaloo!

That same month the band began rehearsing for the 11th American tour, scheduled to begin in late February.

New Year 1977 saw further rehearsals and the four Zeppelins looking forward to getting back on the road again – they hadn't toured for almost 12 months, a previously unheard of state of affairs. But then Robert contracted severe tonsillitis and the dates were put back to April, when the band took to the stage at the Memorial Center in Dallas, Texas.

Zeppelin had been away from the US live scene for a long time and the audiences seemed more boisterous and unpredictable than before. Scuffles with the police at ticket queues were commonplace and it was sometimes difficult to keep the crowds quiet during the slower, or more sensitive numbers. Projectiles were often thrown at the stage, giving rise to nervousness and occasional feelings of disquiet among the band. Plant: "A lot of times they break up our concentration. I'm watching Jimmy, or the group's watching me for a cue and suddenly a frisbee sails out of the audience; we've all been hit by these on stage, but the firecrackers are much worse. They scare the hell out of us."

But if Zeppelin's audiences were rowdy, the band would often be seen to put them to shame.

MAIN PICTURE

'Cut the waffle' was 1978's musical motto.

Aftershow parties became senseless displays of waste and wanton; hotel rooms were trashed and furniture and televisions thrown out of the windows; motorcycles really were ridden down corridors and food fights were the norm. Then of course there were the girls, and the band's reportedly insatiable appetite for them. Whether or not the stories were exaggerated or true, this was certainly the heyday of the American groupie and such girls would have been available in their droves for a band like Zeppelin.

Audience problems and lifestyle rumours may have unnerved the group, but the series of events which was about to unfurl would tax their combined and individual resilience to the limit.

First was the Oakland incident. On July 23rd Peter Grant's son was hanging out backstage at the band's first date at the Oakland Coliseum in San Fransisco. He asked one of promoter Bill Graham's security men for a nameplate from one of the trailers, as a souvenir. The security man refused and a scuffle broke out. By the end of it all, heads had been cracked, groins kicked and beatings perpetrated.

The next day the band were due to play the venue again, but were late on stage by approximately 90 minutes. This was apparently due to Zeppelin's refusal to play until Graham had given his written assurance not to demand more than $2,000 in damages for the incident. Graham said at the time: "Toughest decision I ever had to make, but if I hadn't signed it then Zeppelin wouldn't have played. And with 50,000 people there we would have had a riot."

As it transpired, the document Graham signed was not legally binding, so on July 25th those involved in the braul – Peter Grant, Richard Cole, John Bonham and security man John Binden – were arrested on assault charges. They were freed on $250.00 bail but eventually landed a law suit demanding $2,000,000 damages.

The following night's show was in New Orleans and the group were pleased to get away from San Fransisco. But terrible news was to greet them on their arrival. Robert's young son Karac had fallen ill due to a stomach infection. The child's condition had worsened rapidly and the five year old was unable to survive the illness. Plant was devastated and flew home immediately. The remaining seven dates on the ill fated America tour were cancelled.

This incident was to plunge Zeppelin into their darkest period. It would be over a year until the next album; a year in which rumours of a split ran unabated. Page undertook a series of interviews at Swan Song's office in an attempt to set the record straight. But as 12 months of triumph and disaster came to a close, one question was on everyone's lips: could Led Zeppelin possibly hope to survive?

MAIN PICTURE

"It was like reliving 10 years of my life." Page on the 'Remasters' project.

HOHNER

'In Through The Out Door' The Hardest Way To Get Back In...

1978 was Led Zeppelin's quietest year by far. For a decade they had consistently gigged, toured and recorded and the vaccuum created in the music industry by their absence simply fuelled the 'Plant has quit' fires that had sprung up since the singer's retreat from public life. Any news about Zeppelin was good news. And when Grant, Cole, Bonham and Binden received fines and suspended prison sentences for their roles in the Oakland incident, the press lapped it up.

In May the group assembled at Clearwell Castle in the Forest of Dean, to play again and to attempt some kind of future game plan. Plant was still suffering from the loss of his son and was in no emotional state to consider a major tour or album just yet. Jones reiterated his position on developing new musical themes.

MAIN PICTURE

Jonesy's keyboard influence can be heard throughout In Through The Out Door!

Both he and Plant had become tired of the live act's interminably extended tracks and the seemingly endless guitar solos. A new group motto was to emerge: 'Cut the waffle.' Whether or not Page felt this was personally directed at him or not, who knows; but he would adopt an unusually low profile for the next record.

Various members, including Plant, did sit in with other acts during that year. Robert sang with several of his Midlands cronies – including one band called Melvin Giganticus and the Turd Burglars! – as well as with Dr Feelgood in Ibiza and Dave Edmunds at Birmingham Town Hall; Bonham and Jones helped out with Paul McCartney's supergroup 'Rockestra' project at Abbey Road.

At the end of that year it was time to enter the studio once more. But rather than head for Headley Grange, Stargroves, Olympic, Electric Lady or Musicland, the band flew north to Sweden, to Abba's Polar Studios in Stockholm. Robert: "Abba were very kind and said, 'Why don't you come over and have a look at the studios'." The Swedish band were very proud of their Polar complex and felt that Zeppelin would find the atmosphere similarly creative. "To trek to Sweden in the middle of winter," remarked the singer, "a studio has to be good. And it was. It was sensational."

Zeppelin enjoyed Polar's relaxed surroundings. "Normally, a regimental attitude has to be taken in the studio," explained Plant, "but with Abba's it was very easy going and the whole series of rooms beckoned for you to play good stuff and that dictated the mood." Then of course there was the Swedish beer. Plant: "They've got special homes for the people who drink it out there, because they go loony after about three weeks, and that's how long it took us to make the album."

'In Through The Out Door' is more Jones's album than anybody's. He arrived at the studio before the rest of the band almost every day and his keyboard influence can be heard throughout the record. There had also been John Paul's 'illness', when he had tendered his resignation but later returned to the fold. His attitude then had been that if the band didn't diversify then they would stagnate, and if they stagnated then they would founder in a sea of punk and the new pop that was beginning to emerge. Good quality music by bands such as The Police, Squeeze and The Jam had arrived and was filling the void between punk and stadium rock. Such music was finding acceptance among potential Zeppelin fans. It was this new audience that the band needed to attract if it was not to become what the punks had been calling it for two years. A musical dinosaur.

Whether 'In Through The Out Door' works or not is a matter of personal perspective. There were some true highlights, but on many occasions diversification is replaced by lack of direction. Some performances were inspirational, but other times the band seemed to invade territory that was simply not theirs.

Track one is *In The Evening*, a powerful guitar driven tune that sees Plant singing with more depth and natural feeling than before. Page uses his Stratocaster again – hear the divebombed notes at the end of the riff – and the solo harks back to Jimmy's *Communication Breakdown* and *Good Times Bad Times* period. The song breaks into a slow, melodic section with Jones adding exquisite chorused bass runs and Jimmy overdubbing a thick-toned solo on his Strat.

South Bound Suarez's pulsing bass line pushes the song along apace. Jones plays some convincing barrel house piano too, while Page supplies a rather unconvincing and messy country rock solo. Did his loss of outright leadership lead to Jimmy just going through the motions?

One of the album's most infectious outings is track three, *Fool In The Rain*. Inspired in part by the Argentinian World Cup soccer fever of 1978 the song features a samba middle section which finds Bonzo in his element – had his mother's pots and pans been within reach he doubtless would have added them to this wondrous tirade of percussive excess. Jimmy uses an octave doubling device to create the bubbling solo that appears in the track. Page was also now interested in the new guitar synthesisers that were coming onto the market. Jimmy often played the ARP Odyssey (perhaps the *Fool In The Rain* solo employed one of these) and was later to use Roland's curious looking GR707, with its distinctive stabilising rod linking body and headstock.

Hot Dog began life during initial rehearsals for the album and harks back to a certain girl in Texas.

Jones leads on barrel house piano again and pumps the song along with a great bass feel. Could Page's dreadful country guitar parody have been inspired by Swan Song artist and friend Dave Edmunds? Edmunds released a single called *A1 On The Jukebox* in April 79. The track features a most brilliant and deliberately out of key country guitar solo, obviously played with tongue firmly planted in cheek. Did Jimmy hear it? The Page piece is remarkable in its (surely intentional) ineptitude. One of the most difficult things for any good musician to do is to pretend to play badly. Jimmy takes this solo as though it's his first outing on the guitar; he's out of time, out of tune and out of it completely. Wonderful! Even on this throwaway track Plant's vocals show his new maturity of tone.

The next two numbers are perhaps the album's finest. *Carouselambra* takes the vaguely Eastern epic route once more. Jones is in control again but the track doesn't feel keyboard heavy; his synth stabs maintain a hypnotic feel while Page inserts track after track of guitar. Here we see a rare studio appearance of the EDS1275 twin neck, normally reserved for recreating studio multi-tracked sequences on stage.

All My Love begins with a soft synth figure from Jones that would not be out of place on Stevie Wonder's 'Songs In The Key Of Life'. Page is superb here, as his brown Fender Telecaster comes into play. Jimmy's Tele (it's still a favourite) is equipped with a mechanical device invented by Gene Parsons and Clarence White of The Byrds; a series of levers pulls the B string sharp by a tone and then releases it, creating the 'crying' effect heard in Jimmy's beautiful fills. This song, with a slight re-arrangement, would not have been out of place on 'Led Zeppelin II'.

The final cut, *I'm Gonna Crawl* is the album's slow blues, but somehow disguised as a soul ballad. Again, listen to the depth in Plant's voice. Jimmy's solo attempts another *Since I've Been Loving You* and almost carries it off.

'In Through The Out Door' was aptly titled by Page: "It's the hardest way to get back in," he said dryly. The temptation is to say the band didn't quite get back in and that the album therefore is a failure. It would also be easy to point to Jones's huge influence – he takes the main writing credit on all but one track – as the prime reason. That would be unfair. Page had presided over lesser offerings than this in the past and tracks such as *All My Love, Carouselambra* and *Fool In The Rain* were fine Zeppelin cuts.

The record is certainly populated by a different style of song and Page, traditionally the studio ideas man, did seem conspicuous by his low key performance. He was even uncredited as writer on a couple of tracks, where Plant had instead collaborated with Jones. Could a rift have developed between the singer and guitarist? Robert had admitted his rage against Page and Grant in *Hots On For Nowhere* ('Presence') and the two seemed to have maintained a distance since the last tour. Is it possible that Plant was

somehow holding Page responsible for the traumas of the past year? Surely not. Reports of the atmosphere at Polar spoke of a sense of fun and harmony in the camp.

A different record demanded a different sleeve. The cover's designer was Aubrey Powell of Hipgnosis who, at Page's suggestion, developed the New Orleans bar room theme which he had sensed in the album's music. Powell travelled to Louisiana to see things first hand and on his return constructed a set at Shepperton Film Studios. The mock bar room contained six characters; half a dozen separate shots were taken, one from the perspective of each figure, and six different sleeve designs were issued, one for each print. Grant insisted that in order to create a surprise element for the buyer, the records should be supplied in a sealed brown wrapping.

The brown paper bag sold like hot cakes. It had been a long time since the last studio album and 'In Through The Out Door' shot to No 1 in the UK and would eventually make triple platinum in the States. What's more the critics hailed the record as a huge success, highlighting its range of styles and the group's ability to successfully move with the times.

MAIN PICTURE

The manager of the Tokyo Hilton banned the group for life.

In January 1979 Maureen Plant gave birth to a son, Logan Romera. Things seemed to be looking up.

The group's first UK appearance for four years was set for Knebworth in August. In the meantime the four Zeppelins attended a variety of functions; Robert and John Paul (no Jimmy!) were seen at Dave Edmunds' wedding reception in May; Page opened Phillips Harbour in Caithness, Scotland; Robert joined Melvin in the Midlands again, this time with his The Marauders (were the Turd Burglars splitting up?!); and the entire band mustered for Edmunds' gig at Hammersmith Palais in June.

Ticket demand for the August 4th Knebworth show was so great that a second date was hurriedly fixed for the following week. The band entered Bray studios for intensive rehearsals before two warm-up dates at the Falkoner Theatre in Copenhagen.

The Knebworth bill went thus: Fairport Convention, Commander Cody, Chas and Dave, Southside Johnny and the Asbury Jukes, Todd Rundgren's Utopia and, of course, Led Zeppelin. The set adopted the 'cut the waffle' credo, with curtailed guitar and drum solos. The band played for three hours and although they received four encores the bulk of the crowd seemed unconvinced. Plant was bemused by the silence between the numbers; a far cry from the hysteria of the American tours. The press were callous in their appraisal; *The Sunday Times* called them "the worst band in the world", while other critics referred to the group as "having squeezed their lemons dry a long time ago". Such cruel taunts wounded the band deeply.

But the record buyers and pollsters still loved them. Interest in 'In Through The Out Door', released around the world on August 20th, pulled the entire Zeppelin back catalogue into the US *Billboard* chart; an unheard of feat. They consequently released their first US single for over three years, *Fool In The Rain c/w Hot Dog*. The band also swept the board at London's *Melody Maker* awards, where they picked up a total of seven accolades.

1979 was seen out with public appearances by every member of the band. They all watched Abba's London show in November; Jimmy attended Paul McCartney's Wings gig in Brighton and played host to the McCartneys and guitarist Denny Laine at his Plumpton home; Plant and Bonham caught the December 12th Birmingham show. Robert, John and Jonesy attended McCartney's 'Rockestra' benefit concert for Kampuchea at Hammersmith, where Plant sang the Elvis number *Little Sister* and the others joined in the finale.

With unparalleled chart success, critical acclaim and public support it looked as though 1980 was going to be Led Zeppelin's year. They announced a full European tour, their first for seven years, and plans were laid for another trek around America, due to begin in Montreal in October.

Rehearsals began in April for the European tour, starting in London's Rainbow Theatre before moving to the New Victoria and on to Shepperton Studios. After the usual jostling of dates it was all set; the tour would open in Dortmund on June 17th and traverse Germany, Holland, Belgium and Austria.
In June Jimmy negotiated with Michael Caine to buy his £900,000 Windsor home; he would move there in August.

Meanwhile the European tour took off. But all was not well. Amid reports that the gigs lacked the spark of previous performances, Bonham collapsed on stage at the Messecentre Halle in Nuremburg. The show was called off and Bonham diagnosed as suffering from physical exhaustion.

The tour carried on with Bonzo at the helm, but he was obviously still unfit. Undeterred, the group began to make plans for their autumn US visit.

August was holiday time for the band and Jimmy took the opportunity to move into his new home. In September Peter Grant announced the group's plan for the coming decade. Entitled 'Led Zeppelin: The 80s Part One' the campaign took in the coming US tour of the North East and Midwest and detailed the proposed visit to the South the following spring. The immediate demand for tickets was massive and a feeling of positive expectancy prevailed in the camp. It was to be cruelly crushed.

On September 24th Led Zeppelin entered Bray Studios to begin rehearsals for the American tour's first leg. At the end of the day the group and their entourage withdrew to Page's nearby Windsor house for the night. A 12 hour drinking bout ensued and Bonham consumed a large quantity of vodka. He retired to bed and when he had not surfaced by 1.45pm the following day, sound technician Benji Le Fevre went to wake him. But it was too late. The drummer had choked to death on his own vomit.

An inquest pronounced a verdict of accidental death and the funeral of John Bonham was held on October 10th 1980, at Rushock in Worcestershire.

Years later, Bonzo's son Jason and his wife were staying with Page in the house where his father had died. Jason: "I was lying in bed thinking, 'I wonder if this is the room where he died.' My wife said, 'Jimmy would never put you in the room where your dad died,' but I had to ask him the next day. He said, 'No Jason, I wouldn't ever do that.' But I *wanted* to see him. I lay on the bed and looked around, because even if it wasn't the same room, that house was the last place he was alive. It was weird. I wanted to see a snare drum float across the room or something."

MAIN PICTURE

Gruppenführer Page!

'Coda' The Epilogue

"We wish it to be known that the loss of our dear friend, and the deep respect we have for his family, together with the sense of undivided harmony felt by ourselves and our manager, have led us to decide that we could not continue as we were." So read the statement issued by Led Zeppelin on December 4th 1980, dispelling rumours that Cozy Powell, Carmine Appice, Aynsley Dunbar, Peter Criss or Paul Thompson were all being considered as Bonham's replacements.

The band were naturally devastated by the drummer's death. He had been their friend and musical ally since the beginning and so any pressure to continue was strongly resisted. "It would have been silly to even think about going on with Zeppelin," said Page. "It would have been a total insult to John. I couldn't have played the numbers and looked around and seen someone else on the drums. It wouldn't have been an honest thing to do."

MAIN PICTURE

Just like Plant, Page changed his image: out went the rock'n'roll gear and in came the designer suits.

Plant had known Bonzo the longest and so perhaps his loss was most great. "It was like staggering away from the vacuum created by a great explosion," he commented. "I found myself standing on a street corner clutching 12 years of my life, with a lump in my throat and a tear in my eye and not knowing which way to go. I knew the dream was over and everything had gone."

Just as Robert had retreated from the limelight after his son Karac's death in 1977, so he now hid himself away to lick his wounds. It would be months before the singer ventured anywhere near a microphone and when he did eventually return, Plant's first outing was hardly Madison Square Garden.

On March 9th 1981, Robert reverted to his Midlands blues roots for a low key gig at a Stourbridge wine bar. He named the band The Honeydrippers and members included Robbie Blunt on guitar, Andy Sylvester on bass, drummer Kevin O'Neill and the twin saxes of Ricky Cool and Kevin Davis. Plant wanted none of the ostentation that would remind him of touring with Zeppelin and so the group chose to restrict their gigging to the small club circuit. Plant: "I didn't want to play with anyone, but The Honeydrippers sort of got me at it again. It was great fun to be able to go out and play without any of the usual pressures."

But soon Robert felt the same limitations in the blues that had turned him towards folk, reggae and soul during his Band Of Joy days. He began writing with Robbie Blunt and this would lead to his first solo album 'Pictures At Eleven', recorded at Dave Edmunds' Rockfield studios in Wales. Genesis' Phil Collins helped out on drums when Cozy Powell pulled out due to other commitments.

The record was received with glee by fans and critics alike. It went gold, making the Top 5 both in Britain and America, and Plant was relieved to have crossed such a difficult first hurdle.

At around this time Robert and his wife Maureen were divorced. The split was not an acrimonious one, but Plant moved to London where he could see the couple's children, Carmen and Logan, on a more regular basis. A new image was cultivated too. Out went the crotch hugging jeans and in came the designer suits; off came the cascading ringlets and in came a casual, more restrained and business-like look.

Meanwhile, Page had been sifting through old Zeppelin tapes to find tracks for a final album. Although it was impossible to create anything new, the group's contract called for one more official record. And although Atlantic would surely have come to some arrangement regarding the deal, Page, Plant and Jones felt that Bonzo would have wanted the material heard.

Having assembled eight unreleased tracks from the band's 12 year recording career, Jimmy gathered the remaining members to his recently purchased studio, The Sol, at Cookham in Berkshire, where he had just finished the soundtrack for the film Death Wish 2. The numbers were mixed and in some cases overdubbed, and on November 22nd 1982 the 10th Led Zeppelin album 'Coda' hit the streets.

'Coda' opens with a track recorded back in 1969. For some reason left off 'Led Zeppelin II', *We're Gonna Groove* evokes the unbridled enthusiasm of those early Zeppelin days. Robert sings as well as ever and Jimmy's guitar tones are all recognisable from that second LP. Bonham and Jones are in fine form and the track wreaks of a band thoroughly enjoying what it does best – grooving.

Poor Tom started life at Bron-Y-Aur and was therefore originally slated for inclusion on 'III'. The rhythm section here is superb; Jones's bass lines are so melodic and Bonzo's opening predates Steve Gadd's famous *Fifty Ways To Leave Your Lover* intro by six years!

Track three is apparently the Royal Albert Hall soundcheck of *I Can't Quit You Baby*, just as it was recorded on January 9th 1970. This Willie Dixon blues shows the basic line-up in roaring action. Notice how some of Page's over the top guitar licks ape exactly his solo on *Heartbreaker*.

Walter's Walk was a Stargroves out-take that might have been included in 'Houses Of The Holy'. This Page/Plant rocker features the massive drum sound that John and Jimmy had created the previous year at Headley Grange. Tight riffing from Jones and Page adds to the excitement of this raunchy number. Once more Plant utters his immortal, "Ooh yeah, ooh yeah".

It sounds like it belongs on 'Presence', but *Ozone Baby* was in fact recorded in 1978 at Abba's Polar Studios for the keyboard-heavy 'In Through The Out Door'. Page uses the B-bender Telecaster for the fills and for his exciting solo. The following track *Darlene* was laid down two days later. With their fantastic natural feel it's perhaps surprising that these numbers – which exude more fun than all of 'In Through The Out Door' put together – were left off the album. Perhaps Page's remixing at The Sol and a new found sense of purpose were responsible.

When rumours sprang up that Bonham had left Led Zeppelin and was recording a solo album, he was in fact in Switzerland making what was to become *Bonzo's Montreux*. While hardly an accurate summary of his life's work, *Bonzo's Montreux* – recorded using acoustic and electronic percussion and added to by Page at The Sol – is nevertheless a more than usually listenable drum extravaganza.

Wearing And Tearing was Zeppelin's retaliation to punk. Page had marvelled at the power in The Damned's live show and wanted to better it. The track is actually more like a cross between punk and Motörhead, but its roaring tempo and aggression – sadly lacking in a lot of the band's later material – send Led Zeppelin's final album off in raucous style.

Not wishing to be seen commercialising the death of their great compatriot, Zeppelin released 'Coda' to no fanfares and the lowest profile advertising campaign possible. The record reached a respectable No 6 on the *Billboard* chart and crept two places higher at home.

Although put together from leftovers from previous albums, 'Coda' manages to provide an infectious and highly charged listen. Throughout their recording career with Atlantic Led Zeppelin had used their artistic freedom to create the broadest range of music; from the hardest rock to the softest ballads; from the jauntiest folk to the darkest dirges. But their best tracks were consistently those which relied on the genuine, live feel of a rock'n'roll band playing its heart out.

Bonzo had summed up the Led Zeppelin studio experience thus: "We don't do what a lot of groups do, record each instrument separately, as you lose the atmosphere of the song that way. Getting the instrumental track down as soon as possible enables you to retain the immediacy and energy. The most we ever do is four takes, and we'll probably decide on the first or second because the feel was better." And on the creative satisfaction of being in the band he commented: "Sometimes it isn't fun any more to to play with a group you've been in for years. But with Led Zeppelin we're always writing new stuff and doing new things. Every individual is important."

Although Zeppelin were together for 12 years, it has been more than 15 since the group's last performance in July 1980. In that time the three remaining members have continued successful solo careers, amid continual speculation that what is left of the band may reform. An entire book could be devoted to Plant's solo career alone.

Robert's second album 'The Principle Of Moments' came out in June 1983 on the singer's own record label, Es Paranza. Again, it went gold and a single *Big Log* made the Top 20 on both sides of the Atlantic. Plant could not have hoped for this reaction. Such was his new found confidence that he decided to take the show on a six week tour of America, where Led Zeppelin had lived out some of their greatest moments. Although Plant's new music was both lighter and tighter than that of his old outfit, the American audiences – and critics – raved about it.

But many of the diehards still wanted to hear those old familiar tunes.

Plant said of his first solo tour and the ever present lust for Zeppelin: "It's incredibly challenging because a good percentage of people come to see the show out of good faith; they know I don't play Zeppelin stuff, but there's always a chance I might crack. But I'd much rather be associated with the new music. I could blow the whole thing in one second by doing *Whole Lotta Love* for the encore." But Robert would soon be eating his words – and admitting it.

During the following UK tour Plant's Hammersmith Odeon audience was delighted when Page joined him on stage for a Jam. But they avoided tracks from the Zeppelin catalogue and of course Jones was not there to complete the line-up.

Late 1984 saw the release of a five track mini album from Plant called 'The Honeydrippers Volume One', to which Page contributed solos on *Sea Of Love* and *I Get A Thrill.* Jeff Beck and Phil Collins also played on the album, which scored a major success in America (the single *Sea Of Love* was a big hit) but was not well received at home. While on tour in support of this record came the occurrence the fans had been praying for: the surviving Zeppelin members performed together in public for the first time since Bonham's death. The event was Live Aid, the brainchild of Bob Geldof and Midge Ure. Live Aid was staged to raise money and awareness for the plight of the starving in Ethiopia. Beamed across the world via satellite the show was staged in London and Philadelphia and among the many stars performing were Paul McCartney, Bob Dylan, Eric Clapton, Queen, Sting and Phil Collins. Collins performed in London and then flew to America on Concorde, where he played the same day. A few numbers in he announced some old friends to the stage.

The old friends were Plant, Page and Jones and the crowd went wild. Although not the slickest of performances – there had been no proper rehearsals and Page got a bad case of nerves – renditions of *Rock And Roll, Stairway To Heaven* and *Whole Lotta Love* received rapturous applause. Robert had maintained that he would never sing *Stairway...* again; whereas once the lyrics had meant something to an idealistic young man, Plant now felt embarrassed to sing his old band's 'greatest hit'. He said of Live Aid: "Emotionally I was eating every word I uttered. And I was hoarse. I had done three gigs on the trot before we got to Philadelphia; we rehearsed in the afternoon and by the time we got on stage my voice had gone. In a way it was a wondrous thing; it was like a wing and a prayer gone wrong. But through it all, and through the rejection of ever having to do 'that song' again, I stood there smiling."

Of course, with the precedent firmly set, Zeppelin fever took hold and reunions were spoken of with increasing regularity. Although Page always liked the idea of working with the others again, Plant, with a successful solo career under his belt, consistently rejected the idea. So much so that the two waged a minor war of words in the music press. Plant: "I do find Jimmy's constant commenting about the lack of Led Zeppelin in the

TOP RIGHT PICTURE

The 70s frontal assault that still packed them in two decades later.

major festival auditoriums a bit boring. I really don't know the guy any more." Jimmy: "Robert took a lot of swipes at me. When I came to the US all I got was, 'Robert said this' and 'Robert said that'. Somebody should tell Robert to keep his mouth shut."

But Plant was not the only one to forge himself a solo career. Jones had been writing film scores, such as Michael Winner's Scream For Help (with Jimmy on guitar) and would go on to produce successful bands like The Mission and arrange strings for R.E.M.'s 'Automatic For The People'. Page recorded with Stephen Stills and released an album 'Whatever Happened To Jugular' with his old mate Roy (*Hats Off To*) Harper. He also got together with Paul Rodgers to create The Firm.

The Firm came about as a result of the 1983 ARMS (Action and Research for Multiple Sclerosis) tour. Two initial shows were held at the Royal Albert Hall in aid of the disease which had claimed bassist Ronnie Lane of The Faces. Page guested at the London shows, playing his theme from Death Wish 2 and performing a moving version of *Stairway To Heaven*. However this time there were no vocals. Page: "Nobody could sing it but Robert, it wouldn't be right. I did compose the music so I felt I could play it. Doing that was wonderfully emotional."

The ARMS concerts soon became the ARMS tour and featured such great names as Eric Clapton, Jeff Beck, Joe Cocker and Stones members Ron Wood and Charlie Watts. During the US shows Paul Rodgers provided the vocals for Jimmy's set and the two quickly saw the potential in working together. The Firm was formed around a nucleus of Rodgers, Page, Roy Harper's bassist Tony Franklin and Chris Slade (ex-Dave Gilmour) on drums.

A short tour was arranged and the band entered the studio to record their debut album. The tour, which began in Stockholm on November 29th 1984 and ended 10 days later at London's Hammersmith Odeon, was a roaring success. The combination of Page's guitar and Rodgers' smooth and powerful vocals worked perfectly. The eponymously titled album was released in February of the next year and made the Top 20 on both sides of the Atlantic. A single, *Radioactive* was released and a sellout US tour saw 'The Firm' go gold in that country. But when the band returned to play Britain's larger venues, such as Birmingham NEC and Wembley Arena, the shows were somewhat under-subscribed.

As good a live act as this band were, the fans wanted Zeppelin. But like Plant, now Page was looking for success on his own terms. "It would have been the easiest thing in the world to play old hits from Led Zeppelin or Bad Company," said Jimmy at the time. "That wasn't our idea; we want to prove ourselves as The Firm. We can't rest on our laurels, even though I love playing *Stairway...*"

Unfortunately The Firm was about to go bust. Apparently tensions were growing between Rodgers and Page, and when the 1986 follow-up album 'Mean Business' missed the Top 20 in both America and the UK, the band called it a day. The world's greatest rock guitarist was on his own again.

But things weren't so bad for Jimmy. He had recently found himself a new manager, a new record label and a new wife. He also had a brand new son, James Patrick.

Page had been thinking about a solo record for some time and his new label, Geffen, was keen to see it completed. Originally planned as a double album displaying every facet of the guitarist's huge talent and broad influences, 'Outrider' was eventually released in June 88 as a nine track single LP. Musicians included Tony Franklin, Durban Laverde and Felix Krish. Vocal assistance came courtesy of John Miles, Chris Farlowe and Robert Plant. The drummer was one Jason Bonham. Page was amazed at the similarities in the playing of Jason and his father. In fact on several occasions Jimmy slipped up: "During one rehearsal I turned round and called him John by mistake," admitted Page. "I felt bad about it but he took it as a compliment."

'Outrider' was a critical and commercial success. Page toured the album around America and the UK with John Miles on vocals, keyboards and guitar and Durban Laverde on bass. Jason remained on drums. Incorporated in the set were many Zeppelin numbers, the guitarist having lost the fear of being seen to trade on past glories.

During this same year Plant released his fifth solo album 'Now And Zen'. The previous record, 'Shaken N' Stirred' had fared no better than The Firm's 'Mean Business' and so Plant had kept his head down for a year or so. But the new record was different. Robert had received a demo tape from Virgin Music featuring a production team called Act Of War. The music intrigued the singer and he teamed up with its creators, Dave Barrett and Phil Johnstone. The three were joined by guitarist Dougie Boyle, bass player Phil Scragg and drummer Chris Blackwell and an album was soon complete. Page was invited to play solos on two of the tracks.

Since the beginning of the sampling craze, where recognisable sections are lifted from famous songs and inserted into new tracks, Led Zeppelin have remained consistent victims. On 'Now And Zen' Plant decided to beat the samplers at their own game. Robert: "It was a chance to get my own back on The Beastie Boys. I used *The Ocean* because they'd used it on *She's Crafty*. When Jimmy did the solo on *Tall Cool One* I'd yet to layer on the samples. When we played it back to him I wished I'd had a camera to catch his expression. I wasn't taking the piss; just showing that these were the mightiest riffs the world has ever heard."

Due to the success of 'Now And Zen' Plant took the album on a world tour. As with Page, Robert began inserting more and more Zeppelin numbers into the set and was stunned by the audiences' reaction. "I guess I am eating a sizeable proportion of my own words," he admitted. "But these are great songs and I think enough time has now elapsed. Some of them are sacred still, but if I want to romp through *Misty Mountain Hop* again, well it's my prerogative."

But despite the personal achievements of both ex-Zeppelin members, calls for their reunion persisted. It wasn't long coming. And this reunion proved to be the closest thing in the mortal world to the original band line-up playing together again.

Atlantic Records' 40th Anniversary party was held at Madison Square Garden on May 14th 1988, when Plant, Page, Jones and Bonham took to the stage once more. Of course it was Jason, not John, but the audience reaction to the gig – scrappy and untogether as it was – took the group by surprise. As Plant commented: "The night before at rehearsal it had been spectacular. What happened on the night? I can't tell you. But a lot of people thought they saw something great." Jimmy also found the event musically disappointing: "A huge amount of reasoning for doing the Atlantic show was to make up for the shortcomings of Live Aid," he maintained. "And at the end of the day we still couldn't win. It's a shame, because those rehearsals in New York showed just how good we could be."

In 1989 came Plant's best album since Led Zeppelin. 'Manic Nirvana' sounded strong, fresh and confident and when the singer took the album on tour he included even more Zep songs in the set. There was even a backdrop screen showing clips from 'The Song Remains The Same'.

The next year Robert was awarded the Silver Clef for 'outstanding contributions to British music'. As Plant showed his trophy to the crowds at the Knebworth award winners' concert he said: "This little award was given to me last week, not for anything that I've particularly done, but for what happened between 1966, when I made my first record, and today. I've been working with these guys for four years and it's been a wonderful time, and I owe a good portion of this to the chaps behind me. I also owe a major portion of this to my good friend who has just joined me on stage: Jimmy Page." The audience was ecstatic; even more so when the band launched into the first ever live performance of *Wearing And Tearing.*

Pals once more, had the barriers preventing Robert and Jimmy from working together again finally been removed?

In 1990 the entire Led Zeppelin back catalogue was given a massive boost. The band were in the spotlight (and the charts) again and the old speculations were rife. Would Plant, Page and Jones at last get back together?

Atlantic Records had approached Jimmy with the idea of remastering the original tapes for CD. Of course compact discs existed of the Zeppelin albums, but Page had always been unhappy with their quality, stating that they were done using "bad sounding tapes". So in May of that year Jimmy spent a week in New York's Sterling Studios with engineer George Marino.

The result was 'Remasters', released on October 15th 1990 as a 26 track double album, CD and cassette. This was a Europe only issue, timed perfectly for the lucrative Christmas market. 'Led Zeppelin' followed a fortnight later. This, the ultimate collection of the band's studio material, consisted of a box set of six albums, four CDs or four cassettes. Page also took the opportunity to alter the albums' track running orders. A question mark had long existed in some people's minds over the order of the songs on the original records; many felt it lacked dynamics, seemed haphazard and thought the albums could be made more exciting and at the same time more listener friendly with some changes.

Two years later the remaining 31 tracks were

remastered by Page and included on 'Led Zeppelin Boxed Set 2'. As Page described it: "The idea was to do a second set and then represent each album in remastered form individually. There is one new track this time. *Baby Come Home* is an old blues number we'd tried on the first album sessions; the tape had been lost for years but mysteriously turned up. Robert's singing is excellent; he's just flying on it."
Jimmy's work was received with almost unanimous praise. Although certain tracks had been left out, the inclusion of numbers such as *Travelling Riverside Blues* and *White Summer/Black Mountain Side*, both from 1969 BBC sessions, was a real joy to Zep fans. And Page's affectionate amalgamation of *Moby Dick* and *Bonzo's Montreux* provides a fitting tribute to the drummer.

Page was rightly pleased with the work. "Of course I'm glad the music has stood the test of time," he affirmed. "Sitting there listening to it all was like reliving 10 years of my life. Obviously a lot of memories came back. The essence of it all though is in the resequencing of the track listing, that whole 'same pictures in a different frame' ethic."

Jones was similarly impressed. "Well, it all stands up doesn't it," he said. "Led Zeppelin was the common ground between four individual musicians. We all had different, very wide ranging musical tastes and the space between us, the area in the middle, was Led Zeppelin. It was the best bloody band there was!"

TOP LEFT PICTURE

"Maybe if they can see a cock through a pair of trousers, then that must make you a sex symbol."

In 1993 Plant and Page both had solo projects out. Robert released arguably his best solo record of all, 'Fate Of Nations', while Jimmy irked Plant by collaborating with the singer's arch rival, ex-Whitesnake vocalist David Coverdale. Plant spoke dismissively of Coverdale, who he had always considered a clone of himself: "You've got to laugh and say, 'Good old David'. I thought he was Paul Rodgers but he's not, he's me. Maybe next year he'll be Paul Rodgers." And he said of the Coverdale Page project: "This is my game and Jimmy's got his game. As long as he's happy I don't give a hoot who he's working with."

Plant's 'Fate Of Nations' harks back to the singer's West Coast influences. He decided to use new musicians and the record contains contributions from masters of their art, guitarists Richard Thompson and Francis Dunnery. 'Fate Of Nations' features a very textured production and comes across as highly musical. The record gained a deserved No 6 in the UK album chart and spawned a surprise hit single, in the form of Robert's cover of the folk song *If I Were A Carpenter.*

The Coverdale Page collaboration produced one good album, predictably titled 'Coverdale Page'. The songs harked back to the riffy side of Zeppelin but the production owed more to the modern rock of Whitesnake and Def Leppard. The album pipped 'Fate Of Nations' at No 4 on the UK chart but after a short Japanese tour the proposed US outing was cancelled. Problems aside, Page seemed to enjoy his get together with Coverdale. "We've worked out a great set and I'm enjoying working on the Whitesnake songs," he enthused. "And David is excellent. Right from the start if there was anything one of us felt uncomfortable about playing, we didn't try it. As for the cancellation of

the US tour, it's the powers that be, the relative managements and others involved."

After the somewhat snarling comments made by Plant about the Coverdale Page episode, all prospects of a reunion looked unlikely. Then, in late 93 came a rumoured offer of $1,000,000 for Robert and Jimmy to perform for MTV's Unplugged series. The suggested title was 'Unledded'. "We said, 'Hey, let's try this and see how it goes'," commented Plant. "We found that we arrived at decisions very quickly, without too much pussyfooting around. But there was never any question of us just rolling out the barrel; it had to be new."

Filming went ahead during August 94 and included scenes shot in Wales and Morocco, where the band was augmented by Egyptian musicians. "I was getting shivers listening to the Egyptians playing," remarked Jimmy. Plant elaborated: "During *Kashmir* in the film there's a close up of the solo violin player. He was so far gone. He was so proud, and it's great to work with musicians who are so proud of their roots and not normally in a position to extend into this area."

Although the set included many Zeppelin numbers, there were also some new songs, such as *City Don't Cry, Wah Wah* and *Wonderful One*. Released as an album and film, 'No Quarter: Jimmy Page & Robert Plant Unledded' as it came to be called, was received with open arms by a waiting public. But there was new friction in the camp, and this time from an unexpected quarter.

MAIN PICTURE

The first Jones knew about the unplugged session was when he read about it in the papers.

Jones knew nothing of the 'Unledded' project until he read about it in the papers. Justifiably miffed, Robert was still smarting from the rebuttal when the three attended their induction into America's Rock And Roll Hall Of Fame. During the ceremony the tension between the three was palpable. As Jones stepped forward to accept his award he commented wryly: "Thanks to my friends for finally remembering my phone number." So, after years of speculation it looks as though a total reunion is still some way off. The song, it would seem, remains the same.

At the time of writing, the full Page Plant extravaganza is playing to packed houses across America. It opened at the Pensacola Civic Center on February 26th 1995. The show is due to visit most of Europe, including Great Britain, in the summer.

Page had initially agreed with Plant that if the set were to incorporate Zeppelin numbers they would have to be looked at afresh, using his 'old pictures in a new frame' analogy. But as the gigs have progressed, the arrangements have reverted to those more closely associated with the old days. Some have even called the show a 'greatest hits' package. Try as they might then, it seems Plant, Page and Jones cannot escape the phenomenon that was, and obviously still is, the ever controversial Led Zeppelin. "The best bloody band there was!"

DISCOGRPHY

Album tracks are described in detail in the relevant chapters.

ALBUMS

'Led Zeppelin'
Atlantic 588171
(USA: Atlantic SD8216)
Highest chart position: No 6
(USA: No 10)

'Led Zeppelin II'
Atlantic 588198
(USA: Atlantic SD8236)
Highest chart position: No 1
(USA: No 1)

'Led Zeppelin III'
Atlantic 2401022
(USA: Atlantic SD7201)
Highest chart position: No 1
(USA: No 1)

'Led Zeppelin IV' (untitled)
Atlantic 2401012
(USA: Atlantic SD7208)
Highest chart position: No 1
(USA: No 2

'Houses Of The Holy'
Atlantic K50014
(USA: Atlantic SD7255)
Highest chart position: No 1
(USA: No 1)

'Physical Graffiti'
Swan Song SSK89400
(USA: Swan Song SS2200)
Highest chart position: No 1
(USA: No 1)

'Presence'
Swan Song SSK59402
(USA: Swan Song SS8416)
Highest chart position: No 1
(USA: No 1)

'Soundtrack From The Film The Song Remains The Same'
Swan Song SSK89402
(USA: Swan Song SS2201)
Highest chart position: No 1
(USA: No 2)

'In Through The Out Door'
Swan Song SSK59410
(USA: Swan Song SS16002)
Highest chart position: No 1
(USA: No 1)

'Coda'

Swan Song A0051

(USA: Swan Song 7900511)

Highest chart position: No 4

(USA: No 6)

'Remasters'

Atlantic 1/756780415

(USA: Atlantic 82371-2)

Highest chart position: No 10

'Led Zeppelin'

Atlantic 7567821441

(USA: Atlantic 82144-2)

Highest chart position: No 48

'Led Zeppelin Boxed Set 2'

Atlantic 756782477

(USA: Atlantic 782477-2)

US SINGLES

(no official UK singles released)

Good Times Bad Times/ Communication Breakdown

Atlantic 45 2613 (1969)

Whole Lotta Love/Livin' Lovin' Maid (She's Just A Woman)

Atlantic AT2690 (1969)

Immigrant Song/Hey Hey What Can I Do

Atlantic 45 2777 (1970)

Black Dog/Misty Mountain Hop

Atlantic 2849 (1971)

Rock And Roll/Four Sticks

Atlantic 2865 (1972)

Over The Hills And Far Away/Dancing Days

Atlantic 2970 (1973)

D'yer Mak'er/The Crunge

Atlantic 2986 (1973)

Trampled Underfoot/Black Country Woman

Swan Song SS70102 (1975)

Candy Store Rock/Royal Orleans

Swan Song SS70110 (1976)

Fool In The Rain/Hot Dog

Swan Song SS71003 (1979)